My Side of the Fence

In memory of my parents, whose love of
natural history was an inspiration

*"There is one quality that characterises all of us
who deal with the sciences of the earth and its life
– we are never bored. We can't be. There is
always something new to be investigated."*

Rachel Carson, 1954

To Nick

With my very best wishes

Jeremy

My Side of the Fence

The Natural History of a Surrey Garden

Jeremy Early

First published in 2013
by Jeremy Early
30 Park Lane East
Reigate
Surrey
RH2 8HN
United Kingdom

ISBN 978-0-9530098-1-7

Designed by Neil Randon
Printing and binding by Poligrafia Inspektoratu
Towarzystwa Salezjańskiego, ul. Konfederacka 6,
30-306 Kraków, Poland

Contents

Acknowledgements 6

Foreword by Professor David Bellamy 7

Preface 9

Chapter 1 – Habitats 12

Chapter 2 – Mammals 44

Chapter 3 – Birds 58

Chapter 4 – The Pond 82

Chapter 5 – Butterflies & Moths 94

Chapter 6 – Bees 116

Chapter 7 – Wasps 142

Chapter 8 – Flies 172

Chapter 9 – Beetles 198

Chapter 10 – Other Invertebrates 216

Bibliography 240

Index 244

Ackowledgements

The text is essentially mine and, apart from a few taken by my parents, the images are mine too. Even so, this book could not have been written without the advice, assistance and unstinting support of a sizeable band of people. My particular thanks go to celebrated botanist and environmentalist Professor David J. Bellamy for writing the Foreword; to Neil Randon for his superior design; to Sara Byrne for her meticulous editing; to Adam Bates and Michael Tucker for proof-reading; and to Bogdan Wiśniowski for helping to organise the printing and binding in Poland.

Among a wealth of wildlife experts called on to try and identify ticklish species over the years, the patience and precision of David Baldock (bees and wasps), Gavin Broad (ichneumon wasps), Graham A. Collins (moths, flies, sawflies, beetles and bugs), Jonty Denton (beetles and spiders), Scotty Dodd (beetles), David Element (hoverflies), George Else (bees), Steven Falk (flies) and Peter Harvey (spiders) were vital and much appreciated. The same comment applies to Eddie Howard for his help in spotting invertebrates in the garden and engaging in lively discussions about photographic techniques. Thanks also to Chris Harrington, the family's gardener for more than 20 years, who played a crucial part matching advice with action.

Foreword

lived in urban Surrey for the first 25 years of my life and played in the garden and the old brickworks across a main road to London. There I could marvel at the wonders of natural history right in my back yard, and on the way to school I would collect wild flowers to add to the flower table for study. My parents wanted me to be a doctor; thank goodness in those days all sixth formers heading towards that career had to study biology, botany and zoology to be correct. So I was well briefed in those subjects before I got my degree, doctorate and a post at Durham University as a don in the Department of Botany. Since that time I have read many books, written 45 of my own and have been asked to pen Forewords for over 100 books, all with wildlife leanings. Each one gave me great pleasure and taught me a lot.

So when I received a letter from Jeremy Early, who lives but a bike ride from where I had lived through my childhood and my salad days, I could not say 'no' to writing this Foreword. The title *My Side of the Fence* refers to a garden fence. Within that boundary, with the help of family, friends and lots of patience, Jeremy discovered the names of the flora and plentiful fauna seen in the garden. He also made strenuous efforts to attract other species into his living book of natural history. These actions are highly relevant now, but for reasons dating back to after the First Great War when our countryside got caught up in another war, of land use, that began the decimation of wild areas across the country. Sadly this often one-sided battle is still going on and the news is not good, but at least more and more people are realising what is happening and want to help, including on their home patch.

That is why *My Side of the Fence* is so timely. It is a super book, a winner in its class. The photographs, virtually all taken by the author, are fantastic and interlock with the script so that as you turn the leaves you get a complete picture and learn just how we can help wildlife thrive in our gardens. Anyone buying the book will be able to keep it in the window and find out about the plants and animals, big and small, which share the garden with them, with family and with friends. That is why I shall obtain copies for each Bellamy household, so all the members will be able to find out what real natural history is about. I also hope one day I can go to visit the garden, but it will not be on a bike!

Professor David J. Bellamy
OBE, BSc, PhD, Hon FLS, DSc, DUniv, CBiol, FIBiol, FRIN, FBNA

President of Surrey Wildlife Trust

Above: Female Red Mason Bee *Osmia bicornis* flying back to her nest with pollen
Opposite: A male Bullfinch providing a ray of sunshine on a cold, cloudy day in March 2013

Preface

Wildlife in Britain has been under pressure and suffering losses for most of the last century. Contributors to the destruction or deterioration of ecosystems include a marked growth in population with the accompanying development in housing and infrastructure; radical improvements in farming efficiency; intensive drainage; and increased levels of pollution. With the removal or fragmentation of valuable habitats, be they woodland, wetland, heathland, ponds, orchards, hedges or flower meadows, many denizens inevitably have lost out.

Given a chance, nature can often adjust, and there are brighter spots in the 21st century thanks to the sterling efforts of such conservation groups as the Royal Society for the Protection of Birds, Butterfly Conservation, the Woodland Trust and the Wildlife Trusts along with government-funded organisations led by Natural England and the Environment Agency. Their actions include protecting and sometimes extending habitats and reserves, creating and managing new ones, engaging in detailed research, and giving the public a clear picture of what may happen all too quickly if insufficient people fail to pull together.

Another bright spot is one which, with luck, can be termed unfinished business. It involves no overall organisation, just many thousands of individuals who each have their own nature reserve – the British garden. Gardens, and this applies to those linked to communal dwelling places such as flats as well as single properties, have always offered a resource to wildlife, often by accident. In places the benefits have developed in recent years, just when most needed, as a good proportion of property owners have started paying more attention to the species that come into their gardens, often providing encouragement. Bird feeders lift the spirits of those who fill them and watch the subsequent activity. Abundant colour can raise us too, and bright, well-stocked borders hosting flowers rich in nectar and pollen act as a magnet for countless invertebrates. Home-grown fruits and vegetables are gaining in popularity, a trend that assists bees as well as plenty of unwanted species, which in turn attract predators.

That is the good news, and something to exult in. Not so good is that many gardens in British towns and cities, especially at the front of houses, have been paved over, often to provide parking spaces for the great modern god, the car. Similarly, housing developments frequently involve 'infilling', with gardens regularly losing out not only because large, long-established ones are fragmented and covered by bricks and mortar but also because gardens are not always seen as essential for new properties. Indeed, despite being good therapy, at times they tend to be viewed with suspicion as likely to occupy too many of a busy modern person's spare hours. This is a problem even in Surrey, though not so bad as in London. Figures given by the admirable Wildlife Gardening Forum, organised by Natural England, show that 32 square kilometres of gardens have been lost in the capital in recent decades. (Metric measurements are used throughout *My Side of the Fence*; for reference, one kilometre is nearly five eighths of a mile, one metre is just over 39 inches, 25 millimetres make one inch and 454 grams equal one pound.)

Inevitably all this has had an effect on fauna (as well as creating conditions under which flooding may be likelier) but happily in gardens that continue to live up to the name, a natural cycle still subsists. Moreover, enthusiasts can always provide a boost, though understandably the number of species which turn up depends on the location of a garden. Climate rules the roost in species distribution and a botanically rich garden in Aberdeen will never attract so wide a variety as one in Dorset. Then again, a small city garden in southern England is unlikely to draw in as many species as one in a less-developed area. However, it is worth noting that the detailed scientific researches, mainly by trapping, of Dr Jennifer Owen in her

suburban garden in Leicester between 1972 and 2001 produced records for 1,985 species of insect, 138 other invertebrates and 64 vertebrates including 54 types of bird and seven mammals.

The subject of this book is a larger garden than that of Dr Owen, around one third of an acre, 800 metres from the centre of Reigate, a town just south of the M25 in Surrey. Reigate has two busy trunk roads, the A25 and A217, passing through it and a population of around 25,000. Despite the traffic, plenty of housing and all the associated activity, the garden is in a perfect position to attract wildlife since it backs on to a public park containing ancient woodland with many Oak and Beech trees, while over the road there is a species-rich disused sandpit. Several of the other gardens nearby are rich in suitable flora too, adding to the appeal of the road as a habitat.

My father Gerry and mother Joan instilled an interest for wildlife in my brother Peter and me from an early age, one that contained a strong spirit of inquiry. If, while out walking, we came across species that we did not recognise immediately, such as Drinker Moth caterpillars on Romney Marsh in Kent, or a Corn Bunting in the field behind our house at Woodmansterne in Surrey, there was a rush to try and identify them from the available literature as soon as we got back. This valuable lesson has stood us both in good stead with natural history ever since.

Certainly the encouragement my parents gave to wildlife in the garden after the family moved to Reigate in 1964 led to some first-rate mammal, bird and butterfly species arriving, though there was never any precise record-keeping other than with butterflies – my father was a butterfly enthusiast and keen photographer, interests which he passed on to me. Those wildlife families continued to provide great pleasure to my mother from inside the house once physical incapacity prevented her going comfortably into the garden, and at the time of writing the species counts are 13 mammals, 53 birds and 22 butterflies. My efforts over the past five years in planting different pollen- and nectar-rich flowers and setting up appropriate

A Jackdaw, one of the most boisterous birds in the garden, approaching its nest

accommodation for invertebrates have resulted in a substantial increase in the number of identified bees, wasps and hoverflies visiting and breeding, with a tally for the three families of more than 200 species.

The figures undoubtedly would be markedly higher if the sort of systematic trapping used by Dr Owen in Leicester had been applied, but seeing and obtaining images of living species, along with observing their often fascinating behaviour, have always been what appealed to me most. Trying to ascertain whenever possible exactly why invertebrates are in the garden is also worthwhile in terms of conservation and rounded inquiry. By definition this approach is not comprehensive but nor is it unscientific. Put simply, getting a reasonably accurate fix on 100 species is more satisfying for me than compiling lists of 300 or 400 without a decent factual framework to set them against. Full lists for members of each family recorded in the garden can be found in the following chapters.

When one considers the history of any garden, obtaining these species counts in mine really did not take long, suggesting that just a little spurt of effort by British garden owners could do a tremendous amount to assist wildlife that often is finding life ever tougher in the wild. Seeing a bee, a hoverfly or a butterfly on a flower that one chose and bought as a seed or plug, or watching a bird eating berries on a shrub planted years ago, or studying a dragonfly emerging on an Iris stem in a pond, is something to celebrate, something that creates a feeling of satisfaction, a feeling of having done right. Personally, the whole process has been truly thrilling, and that, along with encouragement to other garden owners maybe to follow the same path, is what I hope to convey in this book.

There is not enough space to do more than dip into the life cycles of all the creatures seen on the premises in the last half-century, or to show everything that has been photographed. My catch-all photography of them started only in 2005 anyway, soon after I moved back to the property to allow my mother to stay in it until her death in 2011. However, a high proportion is pictured, confirming not only how varied and beautiful our wildlife is but also how nature can respond if we give it a chance.

Chapter 1
Habitats

The habitats in a garden, and the species which occupy them, depend to a large extent on geology, climate and, last but not least, human intervention. Reigate has three different soil types in a small area, with chalk on the North Downs, the Greensand Ridge south of that then Wealden clay further south again. With two old sandpits, one now a housing development, within 500 metres it is hardly surprising that my garden soil consists of sand, an acidic substrate which does not suit a number of plants. Enrichment of some of the borders down the years has made them more fertile but even there the sand tends to win out in the long run.

The plot holding the house and garden was developed in the early 1920s and is much longer than wide, 100 metres against 13. The original owners or garden designer(s) planted a good variety of trees, including at least two English Elms (the property was called Elmwood), three flowering Cherries, three Laburnums, two Rowans, one Norway Maple, two Holly bushes, one Walnut, two Grey Poplars, one Worcester Pearmain eating apple, one Bramley's Seedling cooking apple and three other cooking apples of indeterminate type.

After World War II, False-acacia and, more significantly, Cherry Laurel were added, the latter in abundance. This species shades out everything beneath, grows formidably fast and is of benefit to few species. Two exceptions are the scarce hoverfly *Criorhina ranunculi* and, in April 2012 as the first instance I had seen of pollen being gathered from Cherry Laurel, the tiny mining bee *Andrena minutula*. In passing, where species have useful and consistent English names I use them, but in most instances, particularly with invertebrates, the scientific Latin name is applied. The principal reason for this is that English names of, for example, many bees are inaccurate, due first to colour differences between males and females including workers, and secondly to the fact that the titular markings are not unique in every case. *Bombus lucorum* is commonly called the White-tailed Bumblebee but seven other species can have a white tail with some yellow on the thorax and abdomen, led by *Bombus*

Apple blossom is popular every year with *Andrena haemorrhoa*, a common mining bee with a red tip to the abdomen

Female mining bee (right) *Andrena minutula* breaking new ground by gathering pollen from Cherry Laurel

Garden Star-of-Bethlehem acts as a useful source of nectar for various bees in spring, including a brightly-coloured male *Andrena labiata* (below) and a female *Lasioglossum smeathmanellum* (bottom)

hortorum. To compound the confusion, the latter is usually called the Garden Bumblebee even though it is not confined to gardens and many others use that habitat.

Over the years a number of the trees just mentioned have departed, be it through age or through wind including the storm of October 1987, but the garden remains tolerably well wooded, which favours birds. The only tree freshly planted back in 1964 was a Horsechestnut from a conker my brother Peter had brought with him for the purpose when we moved from Woodmansterne. Structural diversity has always been one of the greatest strengths of the average garden for wildlife and the dead wood from a few of the old trees and fence posts proved useful because this is an exceptional and often underrated habitat for invertebrates. With various additions including purpose-built boxes holding cut bamboo canes, cardboard tubes and reeds, some of this wood has been used since 2007 to offer nesting opportunities for sundry small species led by bees and wasps, as Chapter 6 and Chapter 7 show in more detail. These plus beetles and flies are families that most wildlife gardening books – and dozens have been

The wilderness that was the garden in 1964 when the Earlys moved in. Top, my father having a bonfire near the end of the garden. Bottom, the view from the back bedroom. Photos by Joan Early. Opposite, the same views nearly 50 years on, with both sections looking altogether more ordered

Crocuses and Japanese Quince (Japonica) provide queen bumblebees with a crucial supply of nectar early in the season. The bee in the Crocus (top) is a Buff-tailed Bumblebee *Bombus terrestris* and the one on Japonica (above) is a Red-tailed Bumblebee *Bombus lapidarius*

Bluebells are good for bumblebees, early solitary bees and some flies, including this *Eupeodes luniger* hoverfly

published in the last 20 years – treat briefly or simply ignore. Such an approach says little for the science of the authors but plenty for their realism given how fast, elusive and hard to identify so many of the species are.

The earliest artificial structure to support wildlife in the garden was a stone birdbath, which still draws in not just birds but some mammals and insects requiring water, especially in dry summers. The next new aids were a bird table in the 1970s, a smallish pond in 1982 and two nest boxes for birds which my parents tried in the late 1980s but which, for one reason or another, proved unsuccessful. Since the initial bird table was installed there has been a constant supply of peanuts and seeds available in up to five containers to attract and sustain the avian population. The pond has proved beneficial for birds and mammals but more importantly, together with an adjacent concealed pile of bricks and stones to give cover and secure space for hibernation, it has provided opportunities for a suite of wildlife that previously had lacked a proper place for breeding or living in the garden. This group consisted of amphibians, reptiles and plentiful aquatic invertebrates.

An easier form of habitat creation involved a lack of management of some sections. This included hedges (particularly underneath) and scrubby areas on the margins at the top of the garden containing such wildlife friendly plants as Brambles and Stinging Nettles. Similarly, naturally occurring patches of bare earth have been left on the edges of the lawn by the fences or abutting the hedges since they offer certain bees, including the handsome Tawny Mining Bee *Andrena fulva*, a perfect place in which to nest. No fertiliser has been put on the lawns for over ten years.

Perhaps predictably, the shrubs and border flowers have changed more than the trees over the years and those present at the time of writing are very different from 1964, when there were no borders to speak of, merely a virtual wilderness that prevented access to the top third of the plot for the best part of six months. All this, including some sandy banks and abundant long grass, quite probably was great for a fair number of species but in those

My Broom and next door's Flowering Currant offer bees a lot of opportunities – worker Early Bumblebees *Bombus pratorum* (right) were regular visitors to the Broom to gather pollen in May 2012

days thoughts of organising a garden in favour of its natural inhabitants were well in the future for the Early family and most other people.

Common Hawthorn, Elder and occasional Common Ragwort turned up of their own accord and some flowering plants were retained once they had been uncovered, including Box, Lilac, Forsythia, Daffodil, Evening Primrose, Canadian Goldenrod, Broom, Poppy, Crocus, Foxglove, Forget-Me-Nots, Violets and native Bluebell. The adjacent park has a wealth of the latter each year; the garden has also hosted Bluebell hybrids. Ivy was also kept and Bracken appears annually though not really wanted.

Additions in the 1970s and 1980s were led by Cupressus (Cypress) as a wildlife unfriendly barrier halfway up the garden, plus a number of much more helpful plants. These were Canterbury-bells, Common Hogweed, Cotoneaster, Escallonia, Firethorn, Heather (brought back from a holiday in the Republic of Ireland), Lavender and Michaelmas Daisy.

Camouflage – what camouflage? The Crab spider *Misumena vatia* can change colour to suit the plant she is living on but in the spring of 2012 this one seemed to have made a major misjudgement on Californian Lilac

The new pond had Marsh-marigolds and Iris and in the early 1980s the borders boasted cultivated Crane's-bill, Japanese Quince, Lupins, Oregon-grape, Mallow, Passion Flower, Roses, Skimmia, Winter Jasmine and Hebe. Sadly the Hebe bushes, magnets for bees when in bloom, ultimately were unable to cope with heavy frosts even when protected by layers of fleece. Three Rhododendron bushes

were also put in during the 1980s and while *Rhododendron ponticum* rightly has an appalling reputation in the wild for damaging our native habitats and flora, some species do furnish nectar for invertebrates in gardens, which is where they should be.

In 1995 a Magnolia and another Laburnum were added to mark my parents' golden wedding anniversary, but of more relevance is

Laburnum and Foxglove blooms are too deep to allow frontal access to the majority of bumblebees but the Common Carder Bee *Bombus pascuorum* and Garden Bumblebee *Bombus hortorum* have long tongues so can take advantage

Dead wood and purpose-built insect boxes have provided a wealth of opportunities for nesting species, and for studying and photographing them. The most successful box has been one made by Schwegler in Germany containing a brick and cut reeds. This had nearly 200 nests completed in it by bees and wasps in 2011 and 2012 combined

the process begun in 2010 of replacing all annual bedding plants, which have little or nothing to offer invertebrates, with a slew of perennials designed to attract these smaller creatures and give them something valuable to take away. The plants given the thumbs down, bright and breezy as they were, included Pelargonium species (commonly but incorrectly known as Geraniums), Petunias, Begonias and Busy Lizzies *Impatiens*.

Among the newcomers, mixing the wild with the cultivated, were Blue Pimpernel,

The main back border early in June, showing bee boxes along with blooming Firethorn, Canterbury-bells and Foxgloves

The stone birdbath has always had pulling power, including for Ring-necked Parakeets

Cotoneaster is always more popular with bumblebees and honeybees than solitary bees; this is a male Tree Bumblebee *Bombus hypnorum* taking his fill of nectar

Sheep's-bit is an exceptional plant for bees of all sizes, from bumblebees down to tiny yellow-faced bees like these mating *Hylaeus hyalinatus*

Californian Lilac, Cat's-ear, Common Bird's-foot-trefoil, Common Fleabane, Common Knapweed, Everlasting-pea, native Goldenrod, Greater Knapweed, Green Alkanet, Hawkbits, Mignonette, Oxeye Daisy, Sweet Pea, Sheep's-bit, Garden Star-of-Bethlehem, Thyme, White Clover, Wild Carrot and both wild and cultivated Yarrow. Not all of these thrived but considerable success was enjoyed with a host of perennial *Asteraceae* with yellow pollen, including Bidens, Heliopsis, Sneezeweed and Tickseed. In 2011 Great Willowherb arrived in the pond, presumably brought in by a bird.

Most of these numerous plants are useful to invertebrates, though several seem of little value, despite looking bonny to us humans – Daffodils, Forsythia and Magnolia are particular cases in point, at least as far as my garden is concerned. In contrast to those 'failures', the success other plants regularly have had in attracting insects is shown in the images through this chapter, including detailed coverage at the end of eight superb ones – flowering Cherry, Oregon-grape, Firethorn, Canterbury-bells, Wild Carrot, Heather, Canadian Goldenrod and Ivy.

Mention of frost in connection with the Hebe brings climate into the spotlight. Surrey is in one of the warmest, sunniest and driest parts of Britain, as drought orders imposed in the Reigate area in both 2006 and 2012 testify. The mildness is exemplified by the mean daily minimum temperature in the coldest month, January, remaining above freezing point and the mean daily maximum temperature in the warmest month, July, being around 20C.

Meteorological experts claim that this situation will almost certainly change based on calculations about how much the world climate is likely to warm over the next few decades. The seven warmest years on record in Britain have all occurred since 2000 and the Meteorological Office has predicted that annual mean temperatures may rise by more than 2C up to the middle of the century. As a result, the suitable season for wildlife is now tending to be longer, with spring seemingly coming earlier and being progressively milder, as happened in April 2011 and March 2012, and autumns also warmer, as in October 2011. There is still a balance though. The mild spring in 2011 was followed by a relatively cool and damp summer, and after a heady March in 2012, April, May, June and July were among the wettest on record and colder as well as windier than usual. March 2013 was one of the coldest in the last 100 years.

The prevailing warmth inevitably has a bearing on the number of species of flora and fauna which can exist comfortably in Surrey. If the predicted increase in temperatures to 2050 proves correct, this development may well increase the tally, with the potential for colonisation by some species present in France for instance. There are already quite significantly higher numbers of invertebrates in Surrey and the adjacent counties than further north and this gives the enthusiastic garden owner a greater chance of encouraging species into his or her 'patch'. However, there is a downside, since exceedingly dry and hot summers with a succession of days having temperatures of 30C or higher do not necessarily favour even sun-loving species such as bees and wasps.

The habitual warmth associated with Surrey does not, of course, preclude severe cold snaps since Britain has a maritime climate which, though essentially flowing from the relatively mild and moist Atlantic, can come under the influence of pressure systems in any quarter including Scandinavia and points east. Undoubtedly such bitter periods are fewer and further between than formerly – the winters of 1947 and 1962-3 were both incredibly cold for many weeks and 1978-9, 1981-2 and January 1987 were all decidedly snowy.

But we can still get caught and in 2010 there were falls of 20 centimetres of snow in Reigate in January and in December. With the accompanying sub-zero temperatures and difficulties in foraging, these deposits gave wildlife, chiefly birds and mammals, a

Escallonia always produces plentiful blossom and draws in a formidable number of insects

Crane's-bill and Bidens produce plenty of nectar and pollen. Bidens in particular attracts a wide variety of invertebrates such as the impressive male hoverfly *Volucella pellucens* (below)

problematical time, though with certain species of bird the number of feeders in gardens in the modern era must act as a palliative which was not present in, say, 1962-3. Invertebrates and, providing they have chosen their spot carefully, amphibians and reptiles are not affected at all by such conditions since they should be well out of the way in a state of dormancy.

SPECIES OF PLANT RECORDED

Autumn Hawkbit *Scorzoneroides autumnalis*
Bidens *Bidens ferulifolia*
Bluebell *Hyancinthoides non-scripta*
Bluebell hybrid *Hyacinthoides x massartiana*
Box *Buxus sempervirens*
Bracken *Pteridium aquilinum*
Bramble *Rubus fruticosus* agg.
Bramley's Seedling *Malus domestica* cultivar
Broad-leaved Everlasting-pea *Lathyrus latifolius*
Broom *Cytisus scoparius*
Californian Lilac *Ceanothus* sp
Canadian Goldenrod *Solidago canadensis*
Canterbury-bell *Campanula medium*
Cat's-ear *Hypochaeris radicata*
Cherry *Prunus* spp
Cherry Laurel *Prunus laurocerasus*
Common Bird's-foot-trefoil *Lotus corniculatus*
Common Dog-violet *Viola riviniana*
Common Duckweed *Lemna minor*
Common Fleabane *Pulicaria dysenterica*
Common Hogweed *Heracleum sphondylium*
Common Knapweed *Centaurea nigra*
Common (Stinging) Nettle *Urtica dioica*
Common Ragwort *Senecio jacobaea*
Common Sorrel *Rumex acetosa*
Cotoneaster *Cotoneaster* sp
Crane's-bill *Geranium* spp
Crocus *Crocus* spp
Daffodil *Narcissus* spp
Elder *Sambucus nigra*
English Elm *Ulmus procera*
Escallonia 'Apple Blossom' *Escallonia langleyensis*
Evening Primrose *Oenothera* sp
False-acacia *Robinia pseudoacacia*
Firethorn *Pyracantha coccinea*
Forget-Me-Not *Myosotis* spp
Forsythia *Forsythia x intermedia*
Foxglove *Digitalis purpurea*
Garden Lavender *Lavandula angustifolia*
Garden Lupin *Lupinus polyphyllus* agg.
Garden Star-of-Bethlehem *Ornithogalum umbellatum*
Garden Thyme *Thymus vulgaris*

Goldenrod *Solidago virgaurea*
Greater Knapweed *Centaurea scabiosa*
Great Willowherb *Epilobium hirsutum*
Green Alkanet *Pentaglottis sempervirens*
Grey Poplar *Populus canescens*
Hawthorn *Crataegus monogyna*
Heather *Calluna vulgaris*
Hebe *Hebe* spp
Heliopsis *Helianthoides scabra*
Holly *Ilex aquifolium*
Honesty *Lunaria annua*
Horse-chestnut *Aesculus hippocastanum*
Iris *Iris* sp
Ivy *Hedera helix*
Japanese Quince *Chaenomeles japonica*
Laburnum *Laburnum anagyroides*
Lilac *Syringa vulgaris*
Magnolia *Magnolia* sp
Mallow *Malva sylvestris*
Marsh-marigold *Caltha palustris*
Michaelmas Daisy *Aster novi-belgii* agg.
Norway Maple *Acer platanoides*
Oregon-grape *Mahonia aquifolium*
Oxeye Daisy *Leucanthemum vulgare*
Passion Flower *Passiflora incarnata*
Periwinkle *Vinca* sp
Poppy *Papaver* spp
Primrose *Primula vulgaris*
Rhododendron *Rhododendron* sp
Rose *Rosa* spp
Rough Hawkbit *Leontodon hispidus*
Rowan *Sorbus aucuparia*
Sheep's-bit *Jasione montana*
Skimmia *Skimmia japonica*
Sneezeweed *Helenium hoopesii*
Snowdrop *Galanthus* spp
Sweet Pea *Lathyrus odoratus*
Tickseed *Coreopsis grandiflora*
Walnut *Juglans regia*
White Clover *Trifolium repens*
Wild Carrot *Daucus carota*
Wild Mignonette *Reseda lutea*
Winter Jasmine *Jasminum nudiflorum*
Worcester Pearmain *Malus domestica* cultivar
Yarrow *Achillea millefolium*
Yarrow cultivar *Achillea millefolium 'Cassis'*

sp denotes unidentified cultivar (spp more than one) from a genus

Useful plants with pollen and/or nectar include Bird's-foot-trefoil (above), the food plant of the Common Blue butterfly which is also superb for bees – here the leaf-cutter *Megachile centuncularis* is carrying pollen under her abdomen. White Clover (below) is another good native plant to put in a border; the bee pictured approaching the flower is a Blue Mason Bee *Osmia caerulescens*. Big *Asteraceae* (top left) act as a magnet for bees, including these five female Daisy Carpenter Bees *Heriades truncorum* at a Heliopsis flower. The common hoverfly *Myathropa florea* (left) is one of the more striking visitors to Escallonia

Persistent frost is uncommon nowadays and should not inconvenience Red Foxes (left) anyway, but heavy snow, as in early December 2010, is a different matter, particularly for birds. Below, garden visitors such as the Blue Tit on Holly, female Blackbird (right) on the birdbath and Nuthatch (above right) initially were unable to access drinking and bathing water and benefited from help with food as well. Most invertebrates, including in the snow-clad box (above left) with its brick and reeds, are much better placed since they are in a state of delayed development known as diapause and remain blissfully unaware of what the elements are up to

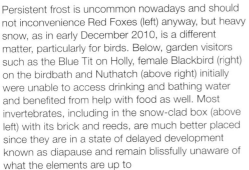

Flowering Cherry

Ornamental or flowering Cherry trees are out from March to May nationally and my two blossom at the start of that period when there is a reduced choice for invertebrates locally. The five species on these two pages were all photographed in 2012 and so far as could be seen, nectar was the main attraction. A queen Common Wasp *Vespula vulgaris* (1) arrived fresh from hibernation, as did a queen Common Carder Bee *Bombus pascuorum* (2). Dark-edged Bee-flies *Bombylius major* (3), which mostly parasitise solitary mining bees including *Andrena trimmerana* (4), are frequent seekers after nectar, which they tend to gather while hovering. A Seven-spot Ladybird *Coccinella 7-punctata* (5), another hibernator, was a fleeting visitor, burrowing deep into the flower head

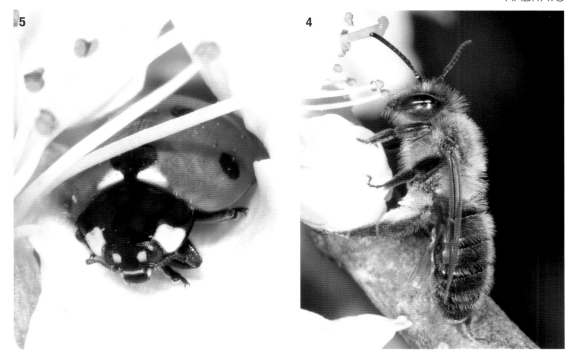

Oregon-grape

Oregon-grape or Mahonia generally is described as a winter-flowering shrub but mine never blooms until late March or April. Bees and hoverflies are the principal beneficiaries and the five species shown here all turned up in the space of a week in 2012. Male Red Mason Bees *Osmia bicornis* (1) were by far the commonest visitors, and nectar not pollen was the substance sought by a new mining bee to the garden, *Andrena flavipes* (2), plus a regular on my Mahonia, the cuckoo bee *Nomada goodeniana* (3). The latter's yellow and black markings probably would persuade most observers that she was a wasp. A White-tailed or Buff-tailed Bumblebee (4) – workers of the two species, *Bombus lucorum* and *Bombus terrestris*, are impossible to tell apart in the field – did have pollen aboard. Nectar was on the menu for the Marmalade Hoverfly *Episyrphus balteatus* (5), a common species

Firethorn

Firethorn or Pyracantha, from the *Rosaceae* family, is very popular among property owners, often being used to create a virtually impenetrable, spiny hedge with the bonus of masses of blossom in spring and bright red or orange berries in autumn. It is related to Cotoneaster, but while the latter acts as a magnet for bumblebees, the greater number and spread of florets on Firethorn brings in a much wider variety of invertebrates when the blooms are out in late May and June. The plant is noted for attracting the rare hoverfly *Callicera aurata* (1) – this male looking for nectar appeared briefly in 2011 – while the small and nationally scarce mining bee *Andrena labiata* (2), the only member of the genus with a mainly red abdomen, busily gathered pollen for a week the same year. Other nectar-seekers have included the wasp *Argogorytes mystaceus* (3), which preys on spittle bugs, and the Wasp Beetle *Clytus arietis* (4), a common species and brilliant mimic. In 2012 a male Green-veined White (5) turned up, one of the first butterflies I had seen on Firethorn and one whose colouring gave it near-perfect camouflage

2

Canterbury-bells

Canterbury-bells flower from June to September in the best years, affording shelter at night or in poor weather plus good amounts of pollen and nectar. Two solitary bees in the garden, very different in size, gather pollen only from the Bellflower family. The tiny *Chelostoma campanularum* (1) has white hairs under the abdomen for collecting the grains and is common but *Melitta haemorrhoidalis* (2), with lots of red hair including on the legs for her pollen collection, is scarcer, found mainly on downland. Another solitary bee that uses Campanulas for pollen, though not exclusively, is the leaf-cutter *Megachile willughbiella*. In 2012 one female (3) and one male (4), with his characteristic red and white forelegs, were briefly at work. If bumblebees are present, a common parasite *Sicus ferrugineus* (5) often is too – females of these flies, as here, lurk then intercept a host in flight before opening the abdomen to insert an egg

Wild Carrot

Wild Carrot, the forebear of all the carrots we eat, provides sustenance to countless invertebrates, not least because the shallow florets make their nectar easily accessible to species with short tongues, which includes most wasps. Visitors include the chunky digger wasp *Astata boops* (1), which nests a few hundred metres away and hunts shieldbugs. Shieldbugs are also the prey of the parasitic tachinid fly *Gymnosoma rotundatum* (2), whose method is to lay eggs on the host that develop inside it. This is a nationally rare species but is found readily in Surrey and Sussex. To complete the circle, the sparkling *Hedychridium roseum* (3) is a cuckoo wasp which targets *Astata boops*. The sizeable ichneumon wasp *Ichneumon xanthorius* (4) – this is a male – parasitises moth caterpillars and yet another parasitic wasp, *Gasteruption assectator* (5), deals with solitary bee species including yellow-faced bees *Hylaeus*

Heather

Heather provides opportunities for a wide range of species. Those taking nectar annually include the butterflies Holly Blue (1), Gatekeeper and Meadow Brown plus moths and plenty of hoverflies. The flowers also bring in bees, including social ones such as the pictured male White-tailed Bumblebee *Bombus lucorum* (2) and a couple of solitary bees that take pollen only from this plant. The main collector is *Colletes succinctus* (3), a species which nests across the road in the disused sandpit. Bees are the prey of the digger wasp *Cerceris rybyensis* (4), which hunts in the garden and also nests in the sandpit, while the nature of Heather allows any number of spiders, led by the Garden Spider, to construct their webs and do very well from flies, bees and even wasps. In 2011 a German Wasp (5) put the boot on the other foot by persistently 'buzzing' the spider on to the margins then pilfering her prey with impunity

Canadian Goldenrod

Canadian Goldenrod is from the *Asteraceae* family and is terribly invasive when let loose in the wild. However, in gardens it is an excellent late-summer resource for a number of invertebrates. Four of the visitors shown here were looking for nectar while the other was gathering pollen. The two wasps are a female *Ancistrocerus gazella* (1), a mason wasp that appears every year in the garden but has never been seen to nest, and a jet black female spider-hunting wasp *Anoplius nigerrimus* (2), a common species on the plot which has nested nearly every year including in soil and dead wood. The large and noisy hoverfly *Volucella inanis* (3) is a superb wasp mimic and breeds in social wasp nests. The male solitary bee *Lasioglossum calceatum* (4) is one of the more colourful of the genus and is often seen, while the female Daisy Carpenter Bee *Heriades truncorum* (5), which uses only yellow Aster flowers for pollen, is gathering vigorously to stock her nest up the garden

Ivy

Ivy grows phenomenally fast but, while not to be encouraged on walls due to the damage it can do to mortar, the plant poses no threat to trees and is tremendously useful as a source of nectar and pollen in September and October when these generally are unavailable elsewhere. Hornets are often to be seen taking nectar and hunting, with social wasps and bees the focus of attention – the pictured worker (1) has a German wasp in her jaws. Females of the solitary mining bee *Colletes hederae* (2), first found in Surrey by me in 2007, take pollen only from this plant. Hoverflies too find the flowers attractive and on a sunny day in September 2012 no fewer than 13 different species visited, led by a new one for the garden, the striking and quite scarce *Sericomyia silentis* (3, a male). *Helophilus pendulus* (4, a female) is much commoner. The parasitic fly *Leopoldius signatus* (5, a male) is nationally scarce and usually found on or near Ivy, where females seek out social wasps

Chapter 2
Mammals

The tally of 13 species of wild mammal seen in the garden or house is respectable, given that mammals tend to be nocturnal as well as secretive so can be decidedly difficult to see other than in passing. Additional species have almost certainly been on the premises, since the woodland near the garden can be taken to host more rodents and bats that might have 'dropped in'.

In terms of size, the 13 have as great a range as any group of wildlife, from 20 kilograms down to 30 grams. The difference in popularity of mammals can also vary hugely, even from one household to another, because they have a capacity to impact on our lives much more than birds or invertebrates. Rodents such as House Mice and Brown Rats can live inside a property, as can Grey Squirrels and Bats – the only bat species definitely seen around the garden is one of the Pipistrelles up to around 2004. Bats are nothing to worry about, though people do, mostly from ignorance or silly superstition. Grey Squirrels are a different matter since they have the potential for damaging wiring, insulation and such like. Squirrels and Red Foxes are able to gain access for foraging if windows or doors are left open, leading occasionally to high-profile but in truth extremely rare concerns about safety.

Continuing the list of generally unwanted activities, Moles can cause havoc with lawns and vegetable plots, Rabbits can eat greens and plenty of other edible plants, Roe Deer can dine on roses and tomatoes. Badgers can cause subsidence developing a sett, can dig up some vegetables such as carrots and are not averse to blasting through weak fencing if it is on a route they wish to follow. Red Foxes and Badgers are also able to root around in waste bins if these have not been secured properly, and on a purely personal note they make using pan traps – small plastic bowls containing water and a few drops of detergent to catch invertebrates – a waste of time since the water disappears and sometimes so do the bowls.

In short, gardens and houses resemble an

A Roe Deer doe making a rare but welcome visit and showing all the elegance and alertness associated with the species

Badgers drank water from the garden birdbath on numerous occasions in the 1990s and tried their luck at the dustbin but without success

Bottom: Being powerful and brooking no obstacle, Badgers sometimes go straight through rather than under or round a fence

extension of the wild, offering remarkable opportunities for finding food and accommodation, especially as there are usually quite a few gardens to try out in any given locality. As an additional example, attempting to extract a disused compost bin from a hedge near the top of the garden in 2000 resulted in my uncovering a colony of Wood Mice, which I immediately left in peace. The species is one of the commonest prey items locally of Tawny Owls and it is one of the most attractive rodents in Britain thanks to the characteristic large ears and long tail.

So mammals are an almost inescapable part of the rich and marvellous panoply in a garden, but despite the best intentions of 'live and let live' I am ambivalent towards certain mammals in certain cases. If House Mice are on the property, as they have been sometimes when there was no domestic cat, they are trapped fatally. The same happened with Brown Rats when they infested the compost bin once in the 1980s. Moles are not trapped but they are certainly not encouraged since they have caused trouble in the soil many times down the years.

Grey Squirrels are not trapped in my garden, though plenty of people follow this route with a success rate that accurately reveals just how many of these mammals there are in lowland England. They are splendid in their rightful homeland, North America, but are not welcome here because they cause damage to trees and our native wildlife. They are also agile past masters in getting at and eating food put out for birds, with the ability to enter supposedly squirrel-proof containers and make light work of carefully contrived means of keeping them off. Rabbits are not

welcomed with open arms either, given their capacity to eat all and sundry, but Red Foxes do help keep their numbers down, and cause a reduction in the Grey Squirrel population too.

Red Foxes generate diametrically opposed opinions within the British public, but everyone would probably agree that the species is a handsome, adaptable and highly effective survivor. They have been a fixture in the garden for the best part of a quarter of a century, breeding most years with an average of two cubs. Watching them, always at a distance, is a great experience particularly when cubs are displaying their characteristic playfulness and unfocussed energy. Feeding these visitors in a small way has been a quid pro quo for their sorting out some of the unwelcome mammals mentioned already but they have never been encouraged to approach the house and invariably run when they see me or anyone else.

That is as it should be – Red Foxes ought never be treated as pets because they never can be pets if most of their time is spent in the wild. Having said that, I admit to breaking a cardinal rule by naming and paying more attention to a vixen in 2005. Olivia, as I called her, was smaller than average, lost her mate to

Above left: A young Badger on the prowl

Left: Two adults foraging up the garden, almost certainly for one of their favourite food items, worms

Above: Olivia on the lawn near the house and evidently lactating. She is the only Red Fox I have ever given a name to and her work-rate was astonishing

Left: A cub at a very tender age – they are darker when born than later on

traffic in March and consequently had to fend for herself and the three cubs she had produced in the spring. Her hunting was inexorable, she seemed inexhaustible, and the cubs all reached maturity. Conceivably, though, she wore herself out since she disappeared the following winter. Equally, traffic once again might have been the cause.

Unquestionably a higher proportion of Red Foxes than formerly now live in urban settings. One reason is not that they have invaded our space, but that we have invaded theirs by constructing ever more houses in ever more locations. Another contributory factor, as hinted at already, is that humans are appallingly wasteful in throwing away vast quantities of food, and sometimes fail to package the discards efficiently. A third reason for Red Foxes living in close proximity to people is that buildings, be they industrial or

How to get it wrong as a parent. First, Olivia (right) seemingly paying too much attention to a cub as far as he is concerned and secondly (below), not paying enough attention

domestic, and gardens provide safe cover for breeding. This can come at a price, since Foxes like to have more than just one den, with the result that, as happened a couple of times in the garden, any and every shed is likely to have piles of earth removed from underneath to give the vixen the space she requires.

It is never easy keeping Foxes out of a garden if they wish to enter – they can scale two-metre barriers, dig their way under the

Ready for anything: the most recent vixen with two of her cubs on the lawn in late August 2011

vast majority of fences or, if that fails, bite their way through old fencing. One desperate difficulty with urban Foxes is sarcoptic mange, a highly contagious (though in the early stages treatable) disease which looks hideous and must feel a great deal worse, given that squadrons of mites can infect the body of an individual causing relentless irritation and chronic fur loss usually leading to death. Mange, sometimes transmitted by roaming dog Foxes seeking a mate, can wipe out populations and affect new colonists for a number of years afterwards. It was a problem with the local Foxes for several years around the turn of the century but not since.

The award for the highest point in mammal observation in the garden is a toss-up. First, and a very strong contender, a Roe Deer doe came down the garden from the park with a fawn while my parents and I were having lunch one day in July 1994. They came to within six metres of the dining room windows and looked intently at a captivated threesome who were staring equally intently at them. Then they were gone. That was magical. Single Roe Deer, always elegant, always cautious, had popped in several times before and did so subsequently, perhaps because the garden represented a haven from the activities of dogs in the park. However, while the population has grown nationally in the intervening period there has been no sign of any in the garden since 1999, probably because they are much less often seen nearby due to the number of dogs that are walked, or allowed to roam.

The two Roe Deer on the lawn are only silver medallists in this competition though. The gold medal is awarded to a species that turned up during a lengthy period in the mid-1990s – Badgers. The first hint of their arrival was when a carrot bed was dug up and the first sighting, in a protracted dry spell, was of a sow drinking water from the birdbath. It was an amazing feeling to glance casually out of the bathroom window at 11pm one evening and see this iconic species supping water. Over the next few weeks, and the following year, a visiting group of at least six Badgers was seen

Some supposedly squirrel-proof feeders (top) are no match for Grey Squirrels in the summer, when these invasive mammals are slimmer due to there being less natural food available. Birdbaths (above) offer a good opportunity to slake the thirst

Rabbits rarely come into the garden because Red Foxes and, formerly, domestic cats have always been liable to snaffle them

Above: This Mole chose to try burrowing under paving stones at the back of the house and, as he or she had no chance of getting out, I stepped in on a rescue mission. The problem was knowing where to perform the release, since there was no indication where the tunnel started

Left: Hedgehogs appear to be a thing of the past in the garden

and, to be blunt, encouraged by my putting some food out. On the whole it is not wise to tempt Badgers into gardens because apart from the problems they can cause to soil and fencing, invariably there are roads close by, with the accompanying risk of fatalities. On the other hand, few people have the privilege of seeing Badgers in the wild (or nearly wild) and they are simply thrilling to watch and to try and photograph, an activity which involved more luck than skill. My parents, friends and neighbours all got the best out of watching these visitors but sadly there was no joy for my two young nephews when we waited in hope in the greenhouse for an hour or so.

Even if for only a short period, and providing they are not encouraged to become tame, Badgers can provide an intriguing insight into the varied behaviour of a still persecuted and generally wholly admirable creature. There was no indication where their sett was – I spent time with an expert looking around the park to no avail – but the suspicion was that pasture a couple of kilometres away, with woodland in easy reach and only a quiet lane to cross to access the park, might well have been the spot. The species can cover a lot of ground during a night's foraging and it must be short odds that individuals have been back to the garden a number of times – one

was definitely on the premises in 2010 and seemingly got on all right with the Red Foxes.

Fortunately the vexed question of bovine tuberculosis, where bad judgement has tended to outscore good science in encouraging notions of a cull of Badgers, is not a relevant one in the greater part of south-east England since most cattle are further west. A minor point, though not for the victims, is that Badgers eat Hedgehogs, a species which can do a lot of good in gardens by eating invertebrates, and which is too often unknowingly excluded by leaving no access under boundary fences. After regular sightings in the garden in the 1980s and early 1990s there has been no sign of a Hedgehog since, perhaps reflecting locally what is a nationwide difficulty for the species. I still leave gaps under the fence for them to gain entry, and

One of the Wood Mice discovered in a disused plastic compost bin in 2000. The characteristic big ears are evident

piles of leaves for hibernating in, just in case.

Domestic cats pose no problem to Hedgehogs, generally steer clear of Red Foxes and Badgers, and tend to be circumspect about tackling Grey Squirrels, although chasing them is all the fun of the fair. Of course they can and do catch birds (particularly young ones), rodents and rabbits, and one of ours brought in a Mole and a Southern Hawker dragonfly, neither the slightest bit damaged. Bringing some of these 'takes' back to the house as a gift, and/or depositing live ones on the floor, allowing them to run under the refrigerator, cooker, sideboard or whatever, was never welcome but happened quite regularly. Still, a well-fed cat loses something in speed, so arguably the impact on local populations of small animals was never dramatic, albeit still undesirable. In fact taking in a cat who had been mistreated and abandoned in 2003 reduced the number of creatures being caught since he had been scavenging almost exclusively in the garden. I saw him jump a metre vertically to take a Blue Tit off a peanut feeder. A few months later, properly nourished, he could not have done that. Put plainly

though, the reason for adopting Smudge was common humanity in assisting an abused, starving animal, rather than any plan to reduce the level of carnage on the lawn.

SPECIES OF MAMMAL RECORDED

Bank Vole *Myodes glareolus*
Brown Rat *Rattus norvegicus*
Common Mole *Talpa europaea*
Common Shrew *Sorex araneus*
Domestic Cat *Felis catus*
Eurasian Badger *Meles meles*
Grey Squirrel *Sciurus carolinensis*
House Mouse *Mus musculus*
Pipistrelle Bat *Pipistrellus sp*
Rabbit *Oryctolagus cuniculus*
Red Fox *Vulpes vulpes*
Roe Deer *Capreolus capreolus*
Western Hedgehog *Erinaceus europaeus*
Wood Mouse *Apodemus sylvaticus*

Smudge with a young Rabbit he had plundered but showed no inclination to eat as he was being well fed by us

Red Fox vixen sporting a thick winter coat

Chapter 3
Birds

irds are by far the most popular, best observed and commonly reported wildlife in any garden, and the group on whose behalf most effort is expended by property owners. The facts speak for themselves – getting on for £300 million is spent on bird food in Britain each year, with the sums always peaking in cold snaps, and in 2011 one firm had 2.6 million bird feeders, 8.2 million packs of bird food and 37.4 million fat balls sold. The Big Garden Birdwatch organised every January by the Royal Society for the Protection of Birds saw just under 600,000 people taking part in 2012, counting more than 9 million birds in 285,440 gardens. Try matching that with other wildlife families: RSPB membership stands at around a million whereas Butterfly Conservation's figure is 15,000, the British Dragonfly Society's is 1,500 and the Bees,

Wasps and Ants Recording Society's is 500.

The proportion of Britain's national list of nearly 600 bird species likely to appear in an average garden is relatively small – the Big Garden Birdwatch involves not much more than 70 species each year – but their presence in the consciousness is formidable and presumably useful. In theory, at least, feeding birds helps them and helps the people engaged in the activity by engendering a feeling of having done nature a good turn. There might even be a bonus resulting from feeding birds, in terms of encouraging people to take a wider view of nature. Only an incurable optimist would bet a large sum of money on that though.

Much perception of birds in gardens is still sentimental, with the emphasis on their being colourful, lively creatures in whose mouths butter would never melt. They are both those things but as wild animals they are also red in

Not a highlight for the unlucky prey but certainly for me as this male Sparrowhawk calmly ate his fill on the lower lawn. The momentary but steady stare he gave me part way through the exercise was both majestic and slightly chilling

tooth and claw on occasions, and always part of nature, not above it. Great-spotted Woodpeckers are a highlight for many garden owners, but they can be tremendous at dealing with the nests of other birds, eating fledglings. The same goes for Jays, and I once watched two male Great Tits fight to the death on the lawn in the breeding season. A more memorable sight on a number of occasions, though equally fatal, has been a Sparrowhawk coming over the fence like a bolt from the blue to snatch a songbird off a feeder. On the negative side, putting feeders in, leading to a concentration of potential prey, can create an unnatural imbalance vis-à-vis predators, but overall the benefits for the songbirds seem to outweigh the disadvantages.

The very phrase 'garden birds' is a misnomer since by and large the species that take advantage of gardens for foraging, finding nesting material or whatever else are those whose real habitat is woodland and hedgerows. Gardens are merely an extension of those, and the fact that at the height of summer birds such as Robins and tits usually desert the gardens for the woods confirms the point. The list of birds seen in my garden contains only those which have landed there – others noted in the adjacent park or flying over, such as Red Kite, Buzzard, Swallow, Swift and Mute Swan, are excluded automatically. There are not many rarities and the personnel have changed over the years.

To an extent this may result in part from my family and a number of neighbours habitually having domestic cats, but more likely the alterations simply reflect sorry and well-publicised declines in the wider countryside. Until a pair arrived in search of food in March 2013 I hadn't seen any Bullfinches for a decade. They used to breed in the park and come to the garden annually when the

The rarest bird spotted in the garden, a Wryneck from the woodpecker family looking for ants in 2006

flowering Cherries were budding. House Sparrows are also missing but were never that common in the first place. Spotted Flycatchers were logged in the 1970s and early 1980s but not since, and Song Thrushes are sporadic visitors now compared with the 1980s and 1990s. Starlings used to breed nearby but these days are seen only in winter and not frequently then. With a mysterious and disturbing reduction in Starling numbers of around 40 million in Europe since 1980 a shortage in gardens is hardly surprising. Tree Sparrow, Garden Warbler, Willow Warbler, Common Whitethroat and Lesser Whitethroat were irregular and have been absent for a long time. A look at the lists in *Birds of conservation concern*, published by a variety of conservation organisations in 2009, gives context to this local downturn. The Red List includes House Sparrow, Tree Sparrow, Song Thrush, Spotted Flycatcher and Starling. The Amber List contains Bullfinch, Common Whitethroat and Willow Warbler.

One-off or very occasional sightings cover a number of species. A male Cuckoo, a species which has suffered a serious decline in the last

30 years, was seen and heard in a Grey Poplar tree at the top of the garden in 1977. The cold January of 1979 saw Yellowhammers and Goldfinches looking for food and in 1985 the pond drew in a Mallard duck and drake – their chances of doing anything on a piece of water as small as that were nil.

The best single sighting was a Wryneck, which spent an hour in the garden hunting ants around a wall in April 2006 and was initially mistakenly identified by me as a leaf. The plumage is cryptic, though having said that, why I should imagine there would be a brown leaf on the lawn at that time of year is a matter for debate. Once the 'leaf' started moving systematically, further investigation clearly was needed. Unfortunately the visit lasted only ten minutes or so since a Grey Squirrel turned up and the Wryneck took flight. This species is a woodpecker but having bred in 54 counties at the end of the 19th century, the Wryneck was down to eight counties by the 1970s, and seemingly now there are none. A few stragglers migrating towards Scandinavia in April, and back in the autumn, present about the only chance of glimpsing one. The reasons for the collapse, which has occurred to a lesser extent in other European countries, may well be largely attributable to long-term agricultural changes with the destruction of grassland through crop farming and/or afforestation. Ants form by far the greatest part of the Wryneck's diet, and these developments have done nothing for ants, though they are still common in the garden, with five species noted – *Formica fusca, Lasius flavus, Lasius fuliginosus, Lasius niger* and *Myrmica scabrinodis*.

Another woodpecker that feeds on ants is the Green Woodpecker, which has been a regular in the garden and nested once in a Grey Poplar in the late 1980s. Sadly this

Great-spotted Woodpeckers gave consistent pleasure to my parents, coming virtually every day to peanut feeders from October to June for a number of years. Juveniles have brilliant red markings on the head but the adult with the youngster has none, indicating that she is a female. The male on his own on a Robinia has the standard red on his nape

marvellous bird, one of the best-looking woodpeckers on the planet, is now seemingly under pressure and is included on the Amber List in *Birds of conservation concern*. There are only half as many nationwide as Great-spotted Woodpeckers, which eat a tremendous number of peanuts from feeders in the garden. Every May for the best part of 20 years adults have brought their fledglings, usually two split between the parents, to feed them on peanuts and show them how to go about extracting the nuts. Once an immature bird, too obsessed with feeding for its own good, was caught by a male Sparrowhawk on the lawn. Great-spotted Woodpeckers have not nested in the garden in my time.

Sparrowhawks are magnificent in looks, speed and agility but having been seen several times every week checking out the feeders in the 1990s they are much less often spotted nowadays. The highlight came on a miserable, drizzly afternoon in July 2006 when I got up from working at my desk to make a pot of tea and saw a male Sparrowhawk on the lawn feeding on a member of the Crow family he had caught. Serendipity was at work (for me at least) – if a female had effected the capture she would have flown off at once with the prey since females are a third heavier and proportionately stronger than males. But he had to do his eating on the spot. It was a

An adult Green Woodpecker seeking ants to eat. The markings are sensational but the same cannot be said for their youngsters – the one pictured right, who came for a bath and drink, shows the characteristic drabness of the plumage at that age

spellbinding moment and happily the bird stayed put for several minutes, enabling me admiringly to photograph him in action. Looking down a long lens at a raptor and being on the receiving end of a brief gaze from those remarkable eyes is a magical moment for any nature photographer.

The only other bird of prey that turns up is the Tawny Owl, a species which breeds in the park and catches rodents, with Wood Mice high on the list. As nocturnal hunters they make their presence felt mainly by sound, with the familiar tu-whit-tu-whoo call, and they have done this from the Norway Maple tree in the middle of the back garden a number of

No hunting occurs in the immediate vicinity of the property but two species of game bird have dropped in, Pheasants (the pictured birds are males) and Red-legged Partridges

Ring-necked Parakeets are among the largest and are undoubtedly the most colourful visitors. The mutual affection and togetherness of a breeding pair is a delight to watch, whether on feeders or visiting the birdbath

times. The closest a Tawny Owl has come to me was when one swooped low over my head at dusk when I was completing an afternoon in the vegetable plot in late autumn. There was no sound – there never is with them when they move – and the feeling was both spooky and exciting.

Jackdaws and other members of the corvid family, notably Carrion Crows and Magpies, are ever present and along with Wood Pigeons – 'great fat waddling Hoovers' as my mother nicknamed them – tend to monopolise any food left out in the open, chiefly broken biscuits and peanuts. Collared Doves can play a part too but they have never been numerous and the way they exuberantly go for such birds as Magpies in the breeding season makes them more appealing than most large species. Anyway, we stopped putting bread out on the lawn many years ago since the above species plus Feral Pigeons, happily not often seen otherwise, and sometimes seagulls used to sweep in and bag the lot in the blink of an eye.

The best-looking corvids, Jays, used to be pretty numerous in the 1990s, with a maximum count of 11 one afternoon in July 1998, involving presumably an extended family with at least two current broods. To show their versatility, one of the youngsters spent a profitable morning on the roof taking

Blackbird anting: Ants are useful to birds as food and they also provide a means of cleaning plumage through the release of formic acid when provoked. Jays are noted for doing this and here a male Blackbird is following a winning formula with his wings spread and a number of ants on board

Song Thrushes and Blackbirds are from the same family and both species are habitual bathers

social wasps that were nesting inside and at least two adults, despite not being designed for the action, managed to extract peanuts and pieces of fat ball from feeders in 2009 and 2010. Jackdaws and Magpies have also experienced some success at this venture though not so much as the Jays. Since the physical arrangement of these species makes it difficult for them to remain perched in such a position for long, their pyrotechnics can be hugely amusing to watch, leading to the question, does the return match the effort put in?

Magpies are handsome and look superb when refracted light makes some of the plumage appear blue, but they receive a consistently bad press. From a viewpoint based less on science than on sentiment laced with a dose of anthropomorphism, they are widely viewed as aggressive, bumptious hooligans who are increasing ceaselessly in number and threaten to overwhelm our songbirds by bullying them, and eating them and their eggs.

Above: Redwings can be numerous in Britain in the winter and are among the handsomest members of the Thrush family, but they are only infrequently seen in the garden

Right: Finding more than one Starling around the garden nowadays, even in winter, would be a cause for celebration. This image was taken in the early 1990s

Small is beautiful – a Goldcrest (above left) trying to find some food on the lawn during winter and a Wren (above) strutting its stuff on a log. Wrens invariably seem to have plenty of 'attitude' despite their lack of size

The Dunnock (left) is principally a species of the ground level so cover, such as Box and Heather in the garden, is very useful

Gone but not forgotten – a House Sparrow (below). There has been no sign of one for ten years, probably reflecting the serious decline in the national population

A Blue Tit, the commonest bird in the garden, making full use of cat hair put out as a possible nest lining

Magpies do impose themselves on smaller birds, but they can act cheekily even towards Red Foxes, persistently nipping their tails. Attempts by Green Woodpeckers to obtain ants are quite often foiled by Magpies harrying them for no apparent reason – ants are not exactly high on their list of dietary requirements. Magpies do eat birds and their eggs, but this forms a tiny fraction of their diet compared with invertebrates, particularly Coleoptera (beetles), and plant material, mainly cereals. Moreover, their predation of songbirds and their nestlings and eggs has had no proven effect on the population of the latter group.

Essentially Magpies, like all the corvids, are adaptable birds and opportunistic feeders, which helps explain why they increased dramatically in the second half of the 20th century to a high of getting on for 1.5 million birds. Suburbia with its gardens and formidable quantities of waste acted as a

magnetic attraction. However, since 2000, their numbers have decreased slightly. The notion that Magpies (or any other wild animals) should apply rules of morality, or not try to take advantage of the smaller size or strength of other species in their efforts to thrive, is absurd. Any species which behaved in what humans regard as a 'nice' manner would almost certainly be in trouble before long.

Crows, Magpies and Jays have never nested near the house, preferring the woodland, but Jackdaws have a closer association with humans and have nested close by in chimneys for a number of years. This can have problematical consequences so they have never been encouraged to stay if trying their luck on the top of the Early house. Jackdaws can be tremendously entertaining to watch as well as very noisy, a comment which applies to the only exotic species seen in the garden – Ring-necked Parakeets. Natives

Above: Sometimes Blue Tits bring recently fledged youngsters to be fed but this makes them sitting targets for predators

Coal Tits are the smallest of the tit family and tend to get bullied on bird feeders. They still breed successfully though, and this adult photographed from my bedroom (right) is about to go into a nest with moss for the lining. The nest was in an outside wall next door and several young fledged, having benefited from a consistent supply of juicy caterpillars (below)

Feeding birds in a garden can result in their taking much larger food than in the wild, as with this Coal Tit and a peanut. The skill of the bird, and the adaptability of its beak, both merit applause

of Asia and Africa which feed mainly on fruit and seeds, they have had a strong feral breeding population mainly around London for nearly 50 years. They nest in tree holes but are larger than woodpeckers, which cannot compete with them effectively, and the fact that they can breed as early as February does not help other contenders for tree space. However, fears that their increasing numbers might lead to a marked downturn in the fortunes of woodpeckers appear to have been overstated based on the success of the Great-spotted Woodpecker.

A Great Tit (right) with beautifully rich plumage

Long-tailed Tits (below) are little charmers that always come in winter, often in vocal groups numbering up to ten. Mostly they look for seeds or biscuit crumbs on the feeders – the pictured bird is eating delicately and dextrously

Possibly Ring-necked Parakeets are a threat long-term but whether culling, which has been mooted, is practicable or desirable is a matter for debate. Two things are certain – the birds' plumage is wonderful and their social behaviour is charming. When a flock was roosting in the park in the late 1990s and early 2000s Parakeets came into the garden to feed

virtually every day on both peanuts and sunflower seeds, with sometimes as many as eight in action. This resulted in quite a lot of noise since they are 'chatterers', but if that was a fault it could be forgiven when considering the affection each breeding pair displayed, and their method of eating. Far from being 'smash and grab' merchants like many birds, they showed a slow and very deliberate style, with a dextrous use of the beak and claw that was almost mesmerising to watch.

The Parakeets also relished the birdbath, which at one time or another has attracted most of the species seen in the garden though seemingly not the two smallest, Wrens and Goldcrests. Wrens are ever present but unobtrusive, often seen flitting around the rockery alongside the Heather and Box. Goldcrests have nested several times in a neighbour's Lawson's Cypress *Chamaecyparis lawsoniana* and are easiest seen, though never commonplace, in the winter when searching for stray invertebrates, biscuit crumbs or other scraps on the lawn near cover. Returning to the birdbath, the Blackbird is a habitual bather, as was its relative the Song Thrush in the days when it was a regular, but corvids, Great Tits, Blue Tits, Greenfinches, Chaffinches, Robins and Dunnocks have also taken advantage plenty of times, usually for a drink. Wood Pigeons are also persistent visitors and the

Courtship feeding is common with birds but not often seen in the garden. Here a male Robin (above, right) is giving a morsel to a female on the birdbath. The other image shows an immature Robin about two months after hatching, with the red feathers on the breast starting to come through as the speckled ones are moulted

problem there is that often they defecate, necessitating a water change.

Dunnocks, or Hedge Sparrows, have undergone a significant decline nationally since the 1970s, with the result that they are now on the Amber List in *Birds of conservation concern*. Given the adaptability of the species, this drop in numbers is a shade surprising, since they make themselves at home in almost any habitat occupied by humans and quite a few that are not. Arguably the tendency of Dunnocks to spend a lot of time at ground level has given cats a greater chance of catching them compared with other species. Against that, although they are pretty apparent when singing they do not make their presence terribly obvious, preferring to stay under cover most of the time. As a result they continue to do acceptably in the garden, where they have nested in shrubs or hedges most years.

One Dunnock nest in Cherry Laurel fell foul of a cat and other nesters, notably a Blackbird in Winter Jasmine by the front door and a Greenfinch in Cypress, have suffered the same fate. There are many more successes though, with the list including Chaffinch, Collared

Greenfinches tend to be seen less often than formerly, when they went for the contents of any available seed feeder year round. The pictured female and male were among a group of 12 that visited through March 2013

Dove, Blue Tit, Coal Tit, Great Tit, Song Thrush and Wood Pigeon. Robins must have bred but I have never found a nest, perhaps a good thing since if visible to a human the structure would be easy pickings for a predator. The worst event concerning a Robin was when one froze to death in a bucket after trying to get some water during a very cold snap in the 1980s; my father never told me, thinking I might be as upset as he was. Robins are always tremendous value of course, behaving atypically in Britain compared with elsewhere since here, instead of shunning the company of humans, they tend to be almost friendly – in an entirely self-interested manner. Get to work with a trowel, spade or fork and there one is, sifting through the soil for food. You cannot help but feel cheerful in their company.

Robins, and Dunnocks for that matter, are not designed for bird feeders, or vice versa, though they do sometimes have a go at those

Chaffinches are still frequent visitors, with sunflower hearts a particular favourite, though most of their feeding is done on the ground. Both images show a male, emphasising the glorious range of colours in the plumage

A typically handsome pair of Bullfinches, male on the right, who turned up to feed on sunflower seeds in March 2013. The powerful beak is much stubbier than in the Greenfinch or Chaffinch

With its elegant shape and plumage, bandit mask and sharp beak the Nuthatch has always been a family favourite

containing seeds. The feeding stations undoubtedly assist the tit and finch species mentioned above when they are breeding as well as in winter. This is not so much in terms of what they feed their progeny as in what they use to maintain their own strength for foraging maybe hundreds of times a day. Butterfly Conservation data claiming that Blue Tit chicks in Britain eat around 35 billion caterpillars each year puts this in perspective.

Blue Tits are by far the commonest species visiting the seed feeders in the garden, with sunflower hearts the most popular target. Other types of tit are also active but the number of finches has dropped markedly recently, which is a great shame. In the last decade Greenfinches and Chaffinches have been quite badly affected by the infectious disease trichomonosis, and serving good quality

Siskins used to be regular every winter so it was reminiscent of the old days when half a dozen dropped in for food in March 2013. Males are easily identified by having much yellower plumage than females (top right)

A Wood Pigeon (right) doing what irritates countless householders – coming in to land at a bird table before consuming everything on it. Their numbers seem to have increased inordinately across the country and locally but there is no doubting the attractiveness of their plumage

Collared Dove (bottom right) about to have a drink

(though often hugely overpriced) food in feeders that are cleaned regularly is essential to try and prevent this happening in any garden.

Sunflower hearts are also well liked by a species which has never nested in the garden due to lack of suitable trees but is still seen most days – the Nuthatch. With its grey, orange and black colouring and long pointed beak this surely is one of the most elegant songbirds we have and was a particular favourite of my mother's. Nuthatches rarely

Jays, by far the most colourful of the corvid family, have always been a highlight. The birds in flight and on the footpath show the markings well, particularly the brilliant blue and black feathers on the forewing – a detail of one of those shed during moulting is on the opposite page. Also pictured opposite, the species is intelligent and adaptable, as one who attacked fat balls in a feeder despite not being built for the task showed. A Magpie (bottom), from the same family, also did its best with peanuts. The Magpie landing on the birdbath (below) confirms how much white is on the plumage

Carrion Crows look much bigger in an enclosed garden than in woodland

tolerate smaller birds trying to get a look-in on a feeder, especially in winter, when the songbird population is boosted by migrants.

Siskins are among the most attractive winter visitors, though nothing like so obvious as they were in the period 1980 to 2000. They supposedly like red feeders but since they have gone for peanuts in green and stainless steel containers without hesitation, hue can hardly be a factor. Long-tailed Tits, truly lovely birds, are also seen much more frequently in winter than in any other season while Redwings have taken Firethorn berries a few times, a Fieldfare dropped in once and a Pied Wagtail was present for around a month at the start of both 1994 and 1995 checking out the lawn for food.

Jackdaws are noisy, sociable birds that often nest in chimneys but not in my pots shown here since they are covered with wire. Cat fur put out for smaller birds, and collected in bulk, provided a welcome soft lining for a nest one year

SPECIES OF BIRD RECORDED

Blackbird *Turdus merula*
Blackcap *Sylvia atricapilla*
Black-headed Gull *Larus ridibundus*
Blue Tit *Parus caeruleus*
Bullfinch *Pyrrhula pyrrhula*
Carrion Crow *Corvus corone corone*
Chaffinch *Fringilla coelebs*
Chiffchaff *Phylloscopus collybita*
Coal Tit *Parus ater*
Collared Dove *Streptopelia decaocto*
Cuckoo *Cuculus canorus*
Dunnock *Prunella modularis*
Feral Pigeon *Columba livia (domest.)*
Fieldfare *Turdus pilaris*
Garden Warbler *Sylvia borin*
Goldcrest *Regulus regulus*
Goldfinch *Carduelis carduelis*
Great-spotted Woodpecker
Dendrocopos major
Great Tit *Parus major*
Greenfinch *Carduelis chloris*
Green Woodpecker *Picus viridis*
Grey Heron *Ardea cinerea*
Herring Gull *Larus argentatus*
House Sparrow *Passer domesticus*
Jackdaw *Corvus monedula*
Jay *Garrulus glandarius*

Lesser Whitethroat *Sylvia curruca*
Long-tailed Tit *Aegithalos caudatus*
Magpie *Pica pica*
Mallard *Anas platyrhynchos*
Mistle Thrush *Turdus viscivorus*
Nuthatch *Sitta europaea*
Pheasant *Phasianus colchicus*
Pied Wagtail *Motacilla alba*
Red-legged Partridge *Alectoris rufa*
Redwing *Turdus iliacus*
Ring-necked Parakeet *Psittacula krameri*
Robin *Erithacus rubecula*
Rook *Corvus frugilegus*
Siskin *Carduelis spinus*
Song Thrush *Turdus philomelos*
Sparrowhawk *Accipiter nisus*
Spotted Flycatcher *Muscicapa striata*
Starling *Sturnus vulgaris*
Tawny Owl *Strix aluco*
Treecreeper *Certhia familiaris*
Tree Sparrow *Passer montanus*
Whitethroat *Sylvia communis*
Willow Warbler *Phylloscopus trochilus*
Wood Pigeon *Columba palumbus*
Wren *Troglodytes troglodytes*
Wryneck *Jynx torquilla*
Yellowhammer *Emberiza citrinella*

Chapter 4
The Pond

The pond is only two square metres in area but eventually added a completely new suite of animals to the garden list

Without water, life is impossible and this goes for wildlife as well as humans. It is essential for mammals and birds to drink, for birds as somewhere to bathe and keep their plumage in top order, and for amphibians, some reptiles and many invertebrates for breeding. Unfortunately, in 1945 there were 470,000 ponds in southern England but by 1998 that had shrunk to 243,000, mainly because in a period of agricultural change, with intensive farming becoming the dominant method, ponds were perceived as either in the way or an unnecessary luxury. More heartening is the fact that this misguided view has changed; nowadays significantly more ponds are being created each year in open areas and farmland than are removed, while since 1970 thousands of smaller ones have been constructed in gardens.

A number of the garden creations contain ornamental fish, which means they are not terribly useful for amphibians and invertebrates. The pond set up by my parents in 1982 also stocked goldfish for a few years until I persuaded my father that native wildlife was much more interesting and important than a few flashy fish. A pond encourages the arrival of a completely different suite of animals, which is a large part of the appeal to a naturalist. Spending just half an hour watching a garden pond, noticing all the activity going on there and all the species which use the water, is not only informative, it is tremendous fun.

On reflection, the pond, which measures two metres by one metre with a maximum depth of 40 centimetres, was not placed in a good position, with a large Norway Maple, a Horse-chestnut, a neighbour's Lawson's Cypress and a fence close by, meaning that the sun has always struggled to get through and light levels consequently have been less than ideal most of the time. Another problem from the positioning of the pond is leaves falling every autumn, since despite netting being placed over the surface some leaves always seem to gain entry. Over the years this can

A Grass Snake moving smoothly through Bramble. These reptiles have been irregular but always welcome visitors

create an underwater mulch which excludes light and makes life much harder for invertebrates.

There is no need to dwell on that though; much better to consider which species occupy and have occupied this space. Over the years there has been only occasional breeding by Common Frogs but much more regular activity by Common Toads, the latter to the benefit of the vegetables and flower borders because these amphibians are tremendous predators of slugs. Since they spend most of their lives out of the water, several small piles of bricks and logs in shaded locations have been maintained for Common Toads and anything else that needs a haven. A favourite spot for them has always been around the rockery near the house since the potted plants on the paving stones there attract a host of potential prey species.

Common Toad spawning occurs in March, after the Common Frog, and the spawn is stringy and black-spotted, distinct from that of frogs. Predation is considerable, including by Smooth Newts, while tadpoles fall foul of all

Smooth Newts are almost two a penny, with the lovely orange colouring underneath always worth a look

sorts of predators such as dragonfly nymphs. Smooth Newts can be found in almost any pond and seem to be thriving nationally. They are certainly abundant in my pond. Adults spend the summer months in water before hibernating on land, often under logs, from October to March. Food consists of invertebrates, mostly aquatic but also some which happen to fall in the water, including earthworms, which have never been that

Adult Common Toad on the prowl for slugs near potted plants at the back of the house. Left, a juvenile doing precisely the same thing

numerous in the sandy soil but have done much better since the arrival of compost bins.

In turn some adult amphibians fall prey to at least two species that have been in the garden, one for quite a while and the other occasionally. The latter is the Grey Heron, a species which always seems gigantic in a relatively small and enclosed area such as a garden. One or more of these birds seemingly filched a number of goldfish in the few years that those were in the pond, and passers-by still turn up two or three times a year to see if anything is there to be caught. Grass Snakes also eat toads but are much less common in gardens than the prey and are a protected species under the Wildlife and Countryside Act 1981.

Compost heaps or piles of leaves can provide the right micro-climate for breeding and I have seen Grass Snakes basking up the garden on leaf cuttings and on Bramble, though not in recent years. The suspicion is

Common Frog near the pond in a breeding year

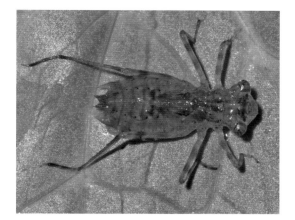

The Common Darter dragonfly normally has a one-year life cycle. Most of that time is spent as a nymph (top left) in the water, where they are superior predators. Emergence occurs above the surface (above right) and can take up to an hour since time has to be allowed for the frame to harden and wings expand. The new adult then has to strengthen up in a safe place before becoming a fully-fledged winged hunter (above left). Mature males are red; females are yellow, as are the emerging adults of both sexes

that they have bred, since in the late 1990s one of my nephews spotted an immature in the pond, about 20 centimetres long compared with the adult's maximum of 150 centimetres. Even though not poisonous, Grass Snakes sometimes are dealt with summarily, unjustifiably and illegally due to the standard idiotic human syndrome about serpents. They can be on the receiving end of more natural attacks by Red Foxes, the Crow family and domestic cats. On one occasion a band of four Magpies gave a Grass Snake a hard time as it was crossing the lawn near the pond, pecking and trying to throw it around until I swiftly intervened. They did not seem interested in trying to eat the unfortunate creature, just in having a 'game'.

The right balance of plants is essential in a pond, as is removing the horribly tenacious Common Duckweed along with any green algae, which is generated by warmth in the summer but can arise at almost any time. Canadian Waterweed *Elodea canadensis* assists with the algae, though it is not a welcome plant in the wild. Plants with lovely flowers are Marsh-marigold and Iris, the latter of which has always provided an excellent launch pad for adult dragonflies and damselflies. These marvellous invertebrates with their breathtaking array of bright colours are quick to colonise a new pond whatever the location or size. Within two years of the pond being created, Southern Hawkers, Common Darters and Large Red Damselflies had all arrived. The

Southern Hawkers have been the most successful dragonfly breeders in the pond. Helpfully for a naturalist they can emerge at any time of day, not at dawn or earlier like most species. They can also get caught in a shower, as with this one. The compound eyes with thousands of facets allow all-round vision and are able to pick up colours, such as ultraviolet light, that escape humans

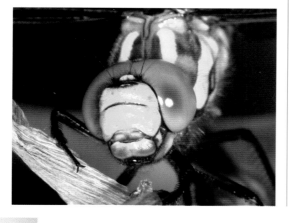

Sexual dimorphism (a difference between males and females of the same species) is obvious in many dragonflies in terms of colour. Broad-bodied Chasers are a good example, with the male predominantly powder blue and the female, pictured on a Sweet Pea stand, brown and yellow

last-named, which has the same dashing colour for both sexes and can be seen from April to September, is probably my favourite of all the species though Broad-bodied Chasers are not far behind. The latter have a helpful habit of perching in the sun, often on canes, making observation of them much easier than with some species, which tend to fly around incessantly at high speed.

Migrant Hawkers plus a Brown Hawker have also visited but have not bred whereas all the other species just mentioned have, along with Blue-tailed Damselflies (shown on the opening pages of this chapter) and Common Blue Damselflies. This indicates a healthy environment since there needs to be sufficient prey available to keep the voracious nymphs satisfied for up to two years. On emergence to become breeding, flying adults they live only a matter of weeks. The nymphs are entirely aquatic and carnivorous, equipped with a remarkable telescopic jaw that enables them to take prey at a distance. With the larger species,

Female Migrant Hawker on Cherry Laurel in autumn 2012

Large Red Damselflies are fine colonists that were in the pond within a year of its creation, and after it was emptied and refilled. Males stay with females for egg laying and adults can go in odd places after emergence to dry out and gain strength, a picnic food cover being one example. They regularly appear around the house

such as Southern Hawker, this includes almost anything that moves in the water. There can be reasonable numbers of Southern Hawkers emerging over a period of a week or more in June or July – they are not synchronised in this. The maximum number of exuviae (larval cases) counted in any one year was 17 in 1994. Oddly, Southern Hawkers can try and lay eggs in a wide variety of substances, some of them hopeless such as rocks bordering the pond, an event I have seen a couple of times.

The pond is not big enough to have much in the way of mayflies, whose larvae feed on algae and debris and in some cases are in the water for years before emerging to breed and die within just 24 hours. The winged adults on emergence are called duns and are dull in colour because not fully mature – they soon moult after finding cover in nearby vegetation. The only mayfly seen in the garden, though on a number of occasions and including on my bedroom curtains, is *Centroptilum luteolum*, which measures a mere eight millimetres and

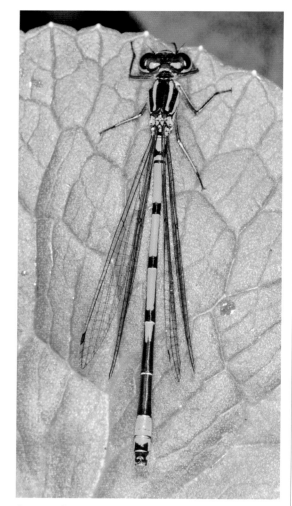

Common Blue Damselfly, showing the dazzling colouring that characterises the family

Poecilobothrus nobilitatus, now named the Semaphore Fly after a national contest in 2012, is closely associated with wet areas. The male, as here, uses the white tips to his wings to try and attract females

Alderflies have been seen only a handful of times

rather cocks a snook at its title by being found from April to October. Carnivorous species that spend time on or close to the surface film and are ever-present include Backswimmers (sometimes incorrectly called Water Boatmen) and Pond Skaters, which also arrived pretty soon after the pond was filled. The former, which can prey on fish fry using their strong forelegs and vigorous bite, retain air in the hairs on the stomach and under the modified forewings (elytra) but need to replenish the supply regularly by poking the abdomen above the water level. They are not to be picked up carelessly or a painful nip can result.

Pond Skaters are a highlight, with dozens sometimes scurrying over the water surface at

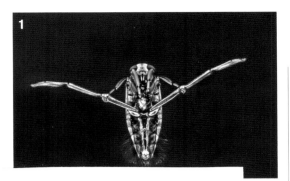

My Side of the Fence

Errata

Page 90
Caption (left) – For 'Common Blue Damselfly' read 'Azure Damselfly'

Page 113
Caption (top) – For 'Pyrausta purpuralis' read 'Pyrausta aurata'

Predators of the surface film, or just below it, include Backswimmers (1), which ambush prey skilfully, and Water Measurers (2). Pond Skaters (mating, 3, and communally eating a social wasp, 4) are probably the most visible invertebrates, with dozens sometimes present

the
he
pond before returning when the weather warms up in spring. They are fierce predators with a powerful proboscis, capable of killing any invertebrate that falls in the water including social wasps. The legs are effective at detecting potential prey and for running fast across the surface film. Pond Skaters sometimes feed communally on large prey, a not entirely pleasant sight, though disputes

can break out. Water Measurers are slim but tough predators who cannot fly and are in the pond most years. They spend their time lurking among plants in or around the margins of ponds, lakes and rivers awaiting suitable prey. When such morsels appear, they are swiftly hunted down and pierced by the sharp snout.

Alderflies have been present only a couple of times. They are related to lacewings and their larvae are predators. The adults, which

The mayfly *Centroptilum luteolum* was recorded several years in a row at the turn of the century

Two mosquitoes getting ready for take-off among a handsome set of egg rafts in a large plastic bucket

Not a welcome visitor when the pond contained goldfish – a Grey Heron, a species that also takes amphibians

are weak fliers, emerge in late spring, eating little and laying eggs on aquatic plants or any flora overhanging water, such as trees. The larvae fall in once they have hatched. A more colourful but similarly common insect found on the surface of ponds of all sizes is the Semaphore Fly *Poecilobothrus nobilitatus*, a long-legged fly from the Dolichopodidae family. The adults are typically found wherever there is surface weed or algae. Larvae are believed to be predatory, developing in damp soil; adults certainly are, feeding on a range of invertebrates. The male has white tips to the wings. They were at the pond in the 1990s but have not been evident since. Possibly one of the problems there, and

Small freshwater snails – this one was seven millimetres long – are commoner in water butts than in the pond

POND SPECIES RECORDED

AMPHIBIANS AND REPTILES
Common Frog *Rana temporaria*
Common Toad *Bufo bufo*
Grass Snake *Natrix natrix*
Smooth Newt *Lissotriton vulgaris*

DRAGONFLIES
Blue-tailed Damselfly *Ischnura elegans*
Broad-bodied Chaser *Libellula depressa*
Brown Hawker *Aeshna grandis*
Common Blue Damselfly
Enallagma cyathigerum
Common Darter *Sympetrum striolatum*
Large Red Damselfly
Pyrrhosoma nymphula
Migrant Hawker *Aeshna mixta*
Southern Hawker *Aeshna cyanea*

OTHER INVERTEBRATES
Alderfly *Sialis lutaria*
Backswimmer *Notonecta glauca*
Common Pond Skater *Gerris lacustris*
Mayfly *Centroptilum luteolum*
Mosquito *Culex pipiens*
Semaphore Fly *Poecilobothrus nobilitatus*
Water Measurer *Hydrometra stagnorum*

certainly with some other species, was that a tree root pierced the plastic lining of the pond, leading to its being replaced. We attempted to retain as many of the invertebrate larvae as we could, but some losses were inevitable.

Mosquitoes have never been a problem locally though the commonest of Britain's 28 active species, *Culex pipiens*, has bred frequently in water butts and smaller containers holding liquid, mostly rainwater. Their egg rafts at the surface are works of art. *Culex pipiens* overwinter as adults and generally do not bite humans, preferring the blood of birds. Doubtless birds get their own back by eating countless numbers of mosquitoes.

There are more than 30 species of freshwater snail in Britain, varying greatly in size, and while the pond has always had its share of small ones, the water butts further up the garden are well stocked with them. None

of these were introduced deliberately although I sometimes transfer some from one container to another to even out the population. There are pros and cons for water snails, though more of the former. By eating, they help cut the build-up of decaying organic matter and they have a taste for that bane of pond management, algae. Against that, their faeces can add to nitrate levels in the water and they act as hosts for a range of parasites. The numbers in the garden hardly suggest they are likely to cause a problem in either respect.

Chapter 5
Butterflies & Moths

Respectable camouflage by this Brimstone on a Daffodil, one of few invertebrates to have been seen using the plant

n the garden, as elsewhere, invertebrates massively outscore all the other wildlife families, and received opinion loudly canvasses the cause of butterflies as the first group to be detailed in any study. My reasons for leading off with them are entirely personal because my father's passion for butterflies imbued me with a similar enthusiasm. Moreover, any number of wildlife high points each year revolve around these beautiful, elegant creatures. Among them are the first Brimstone sighted in February or March after surviving the rigours of hibernation; male and female Orange Tips and Holly Blues fluttering around or just breezing through in April and May; Speckled Woods spiralling upwards courting in dappled light; the first migrant Painted Lady to reach the garden in June after the long journey up from the Mediterranean; a freshly-emerged, brilliantly-coloured Peacock sunbathing on a wall in August.

In short, my life is, and the lives of countless other people are, enhanced immensely by butterflies. However, a little perspective is valuable here. The notion that wildlife species which are perceived as attractive, useful or beneficial should be welcomed into a garden while those which lack these supposed qualities should stay outside has plenty of currency. Basing judgements of nature on its supposed standing as an adjunct of our lives rather than as an independent entity, and paying no attention to the principles governing biodiversity or to the mobility and life cycles of species, is a pretty daft concept. This nonsense is compounded by an inherent inconsistency, since informed analysis reveals that many species widely regarded as unhelpful nuisances, including spiders and wasps, are by accident very 'useful', whereas some seen as beneficial have only a marginal impact beyond the aesthetic.

To some extent this is the case with butterflies, which have an uncommon capacity to make the spirits soar but do not eat 'pests' and, while effective as pollinators, cannot compete with bees or some specialist moths in that regard. In the vast majority of gardens they are too few to be a major factor in pollination anyway, and their physiognomy does not assist in that department either. Bees are often hairy and invariably get close to the action on a plant, taking not only nectar but pollen, using purpose-built equipment for the collection. Butterflies tend to be less hairy, are mostly looking for nectar, and their often long legs and proboscis can result in a distinct separation from the anthers and stigma of many flowers. This means that fewer grains are likely to be picked up and passed on even adventitiously, though the fact that butterflies are very active and visit a lot of flowers helps compensate for this.

There is also occasionally a lack of joined-up thinking in encouraging butterflies into gardens. Honeybees apart, butterflies, and to a lesser extent moths, which are dealt with later in this chapter, are the most popular invertebrates in Britain. The fact that more

than 34,000 people took part in Butterfly Conservation's Big Butterfly Count in 2011 confirms as much. Dovetailing with that, planting shrubs such as Buddleja or Iceplant is useful in attracting into gardens often showy Lepidoptera seeking sustenance. But helping with nectar is merely putting icing on the cake. The key is support for breeding by maintaining a consistent supply of food plants and, where possible, creating suitable territories.

These are rarely mentioned in connection with 'butterfly gardening', which is a shame in an era when a number of formerly common species are declining dramatically. Data provided by Butterfly Conservation in 2011 revealed that from 2000 to 2010 three-quarters of our species declined in population or distribution including Essex Skipper numbers falling by 67 per cent and those of Small Tortoiseshell and Small Skipper by 64 per cent and 62 per cent respectively. The latter two

Brown Hairstreak, photographed by my father on Canadian Goldenrod in August 1988

Black wing edges mark this Holly Blue down as a female

have been seen in the garden, as have some which have increased their range such as the Comma, Peacock and Speckled Wood – the last-named is shown on the opening pages of this chapter. For the Comma that is a real turnaround as their numbers in Britain had crashed dramatically up to around 1920.

In truth, though, the way butterflies breed means that providing nectar-bearing plants is a whole lot easier than providing food plants and creating territories. Food plants are often not ones which even people happy to classify themselves as wildlife gardeners would plant. Larvae of around a quarter of the 59 resident and annually migrant British species feed on grasses, several use Stinging Nettles, some use Dog Violet, others use Vetches, Common Sorrel, Oak, Elm, Blackthorn or Buckthorn. Stinging Nettles, used by the Comma, Peacock, Red Admiral and Small Tortoiseshell, together with Holly and Ivy for the Holly Blue, are not difficult to have in a garden but are never terribly popular, while getting the right kind of grasses and maintaining them is a bit of a

No-go area: a Green-veined White inside netting intended to protect cabbages on the vegetable plot

lottery. Above all, a number of butterfly species require significantly larger open spaces than are found in gardens to enable them to obtain mates and breed. That is why such localities as the North Downs and South Downs can be so good for them.

Several butterfly species have bred in the garden. Common Sorrel has always been on the premises and Small Coppers have taken advantage of this. All those seen in the garden and the surrounding area have been an aberrant but not uncommon colour form with blue spots on the hind wings. Holly and Ivy have done their duty as food plants for the Holly Blue, which breeds annually, using Holly for the caterpillars early in the year and Ivy for those emerging later that overwinter as pupae. Other plants can be used, including Bramble. The Holly Blue suffers from a 'boom and bust' syndrome relating in all probability to the ichneumon wasp *Listrodromus*

nycthemerus that parasitises the species and has been seen in the garden. Occasionally Large Whites have bred in the vegetable plot, and Commas and Peacocks did so annually in the days when there were significant patches of Stinging Nettles. Sadly these were lost in the late 1980s more by accident than design due to scrubbing over at the top of the garden.

Purple Hairstreaks used to breed on Oak trees just outside the garden but came in to take nectar from Brambles in the early 1990s, and with Common Blues visiting the sizeable stand of Bird's-foot-trefoil I planted in 2008 there is an outside chance that they will breed too. Most species, though, are just passing through. The fact that the North Downs are fairly close presumably would explain why a Dark Green Fritillary arrived in 1999. Similarly, although at the time I could not see why a Brown Hairstreak was gathering nectar from Canadian Goldenrod in August 1988 unless it

Large Skippers, from a family which can seem more moth-like than others, are not regular visitors. This is a male, with a sex-brand on each forewing

Small Copper, showing the blue spots on the hind wings which are characteristic of local specimens

Male Orange Tips are active in sunshine and tend to settle, showing their glory, mainly when it is cloudy

had been reared and released, a not uncommon and scientifically unhelpful piece of behaviour by some enthusiasts, it transpired that this scarce species breeds in low densities not that far to the south. Where a Silver-washed Fritillary came from in 2000 is a mystery but this spectacular butterfly was a visitor in which to exult.

The commonest butterflies in the summer months are the three Whites (Large, Small and Green-veined), the relatively drab Meadow Brown and the latter's relative, the Gatekeeper or Hedge Brown. Large Whites and Small Whites do not often settle but patrol busily

where I grow cabbages since their larvae regularly feed on brassicas. As mentioned earlier, Large Whites have bred in the garden. In 2012 a Green-veined White breached the nylon netting that cocoons the cabbages each year though their larvae feed on a much wider variety of plants including Charlock, Cuckooflower and Garlic Mustard. Gatekeepers are habitual visitors to flowers and, like many common species, they are rather taken for granted. But just as with 'little brown jobs' among birds, they repay close examination since the colouring on the wings inside, especially on emergence, is a delight.

Female and male Meadow Browns are pretty easy to tell apart due to the marked lack of orange on the latter's wings

Gatekeepers are closely related to Meadow Browns yet are much more colourful, with the sexes separated by the male's having dark streaks on the forewings. The female basking on dead wood here was probably past her best since the image was taken in mid-September, though the hues still shine through

The same can be said for the Small Tortoiseshell, but having been almost two a penny up until the 1990s this species has declined dramatically as the figure mentioned earlier in this chapter reveals. The reasons for this are unclear. Other species relying on Stinging Nettles have done well and the finger of suspicion points at the parasitoid fly *Sturmia bella*, first seen in Britain in 1999. This fly's eggs are regularly found on Nettles alongside Small Tortoiseshell caterpillars and one theory is that the caterpillars eat these eggs, which hatch inside them when they are cocoons and proceed to consume the host. *Sturmia bella* is a mainland European species, where it seems not to have anything like such a negative effect.

Perhaps the oddest event in the garden

The Comma that got it wrong, with the caterpillar choosing a window frame on which to pupate. The chrysalis (bottom) was taken by a predator despite protective measures. Below, an adult with the ragged wing edges that set them apart in the British list

concerning a butterfly species occurred in September 2012 when I found a Comma caterpillar on the point of pupating on a window frame at the back of the house. With no Stinging Nettles anywhere near, the food plant was almost certainly a small Elm four metres away. Quite why the caterpillar travelled to a completely open spot where camouflage was non-existent is inexplicable. Sadly, despite my placing two pieces of wood in front of the chrysalis to provide concealment, an unknown predator snaffled it within three days of the caterpillar's arrival.

My father's interest in Lepidoptera started out with moths, before he moved on to

Painted Ladies that are seen in June, like this one, are strong fliers which started out in the Mediterranean. They are habitual nectar feeders, hardly surprising considering the distances they travel

butterflies, a vastly smaller group numerically and one that is altogether easier to study since they are all day-flying and on the whole can be photographed more readily. With several trips including to Scotland and the Isle of Wight, and a little help from me getting images of some species in north-west England and the Swallowtail in Norfolk, he completed a portfolio of photographs of all the British species a couple of years before he died in 1997.

Surrey has had a phenomenal number of moths recorded over the years – at least 1,700 species, most of which are micro-moths. The majority lack anything in the way of bright colouring as adults but others are spectacular and my plan was to take advantage of the offer of an expert friend to set up a light-trap in the garden in 2012 to find out what was about. This intention was stimulated by the fact that moth larvae are often much more catholic in

Peacocks visit the garden each year but no longer breed

A rare to non-existent sight nowadays – a Small Tortoiseshell. As with other Vanessids including the Peacock, the underside of the wings (right) is nothing like so bright as the top

their eating habits than butterfly larvae – most of the species already found in the garden had suitable trees and other plants on the premises or close by in the park. Regrettably the dismal weather of the summer of 2012 made monitoring not even worth the attempt. As a result, my knowledge of the local moths is more superficial than it should be.

Be that as it may, one thing is certain – the number of moths locally will have fallen since we moved to the house in 1964. Detailed analysis of 337 species of common moths carried out since 1968 by Rothamsted Research and Butterfly Conservation shows that moth numbers have dropped by around a third nationally and by more than half in southern England. One moth seen in the garden up to the early 1990s, the lovely and once quite common White Ermine, has suffered a fearful 77 per cent decline, resulting in 2007 in its inclusion in the UK Biodiversity Action Plan for further research. Worryingly, in the 20th century 62 species of moth became extinct in Britain and 81 currently are listed as top

Red Admirals are large, unmistakable and seen often enough in gardens to make them one of our most popular species

priorities for conservation action.

There have been several impressive visitors to the garden, notably two different types of Clearwing, an under-recorded genus with 15 species nationwide whose caterpillars for the most part feed just below the bark of deciduous trees and take anything from one to three years to reach maturity. All the species are day-flying and striking in appearance, resembling Hymenoptera. A female Yellow-legged Clearwing *Synanthedon vespiformis* turned up to take nectar on Heather in August 2006. The description *vespiformis* gives the game away, since a casual glance might have led to the conclusion that she was a wasp. The larvae feed principally on Oak or sometimes on Sweet Chestnut, both of which are close by in the park.

Having one of these spectacular moths visiting would have been a cause for celebration but in June 2011 a friend spotted another species on a Cotoneaster bush that was in full bloom and had significant numbers of bumblebees, especially *Bombus hypnorum*, at work on it. This one was a male Red-belted Clearwing, a southern species which flies from June to August and is associated with old fruit trees, notably Apple, in which its larvae develop. Adult Clearwings are not commonly spotted in the wild, they are usually enticed out with pheromone lures, and the majority of the group, including the Yellow-legged, is designated as nationally scarce.

Clearwings are colourful but the most imposing genus in size and in hue, particularly the larvae which can be decidedly bright, are the Hawk-moths. The majority are nocturnal and the caterpillars feed on a wide range of trees and shrubs, some showing considerable adaptability. An Eyed Hawk-moth turned up in 1995 and a Lime Hawk-moth was found resting on the trunk of our Horse-chestnut in June 1997. This was the last moth or butterfly my father photographed; he died a month later. Both these species are relatively common in residential areas, emerging around May or

The two most spectacular day-flying moths to have appeared in the garden – a male Red-belted Clearwing and a female Yellow-legged Clearwing. Both species are showing the lovely tonal qualities of the narrow, mostly transparent wings

Hawk-moths are large and nocturnal. The features on the wings which give the Eyed Hawk-moth its name are evident. The Lime Hawk-moth was photographed by my father

June. As one might expect, the Eyed Hawk-moth has false eyes to startle potential predators. Their larvae feed on Apple, Willow and Laurel among others, so the garden had enough to assist there, while the Lime Hawk-moth uses cultivated Maple and Birch as well as the tree after which it is named.

Many adult moths have superb camouflage but that is not the case with the White Ermine, mentioned above, which mated in the undergrowth up the garden in 1993 and had been seen before that. There has been no sign of the species this century, which may fit its national profile. Quite why the White Ermine has undergone such a dramatic decline is inexplicable, since it is not that particular in the food plants used. Another two of the garden species have been added to the Biodiversity Action Plan list because of a seemingly dramatic decline in numbers. They are the Cinnabar, which breeds on Common Ragwort in the sandpit over the road and has appeared a few times, and the Dot, which uses a number of different plants for its progeny and has been seen just once. By comparison, none of the other moths identified in the garden are scarce. One that might have got blown in from the chalk downs to the north in 2012 was a Burnet Companion.

Another bonny visitor is the Small Magpie, which I have seen and photographed in the park nearby and was noted in the garden when Stinging Nettles, the food plant, were present in the early 1980s. Others to cut a dash during the day are the Yellow Shell, which is none too easy to track, usually diving deep into another inaccessible piece of greenery if disturbed, the attractively coloured *Pyrausta purpuralis*, which

The Cypress Pug is a relatively recent arrival in Britain

In the right place the camouflage of an Angle Shades is outstanding but that hardly applies on a green leaf

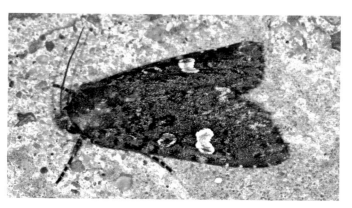

Three species which have suffered a decline over the last 25 years are the Cinnabar (top), with attractive red and black or brown markings, the White Ermine, shown mating (above), and the Dot (left), photographed early one morning on a paving stone outside the kitchen

One of our most attractive moths, the Swallow-tailed Moth, photographed on a settee after coming into the house overnight

Getting a Large Yellow Underwing to show the yellow is none too easy in my experience but the ochre hue of the wings on the outside is almost as appealing

Male Orange Swift on the shed. Swift moths are crepuscular and considered very primitive; the larvae, which eat roots underground, can take years to reach maturity

Plume moth (above), probably *Emmelina monodactyla*, on the outside of a kitchen window

Apple-leaf Skeletonizer (left) on Canadian Goldenrod

is double-brooded with the larvae eating Thyme among other plants, and the Common Carpet, which uses Bedstraw as the food plant. One of these spent a while on the Heather in August 2012, a month that saw a Silver Y sunbathing for half an hour on one of the drilled logs put in for bees and wasps up the garden. Silver Ys are notable and sometimes very numerous annual migrants from Europe and can be seen for much of the year but they do breed here, using a wide variety of food plants. The second brood appears in late summer but it is not certain whether they can overwinter. The Silver Y's camouflage is splendid, as is that of the Angle Shades when it is on the right surface such as a tree trunk or dead leaves. They have visited several times.

Moths are attracted to light and plume moths, which hold their wings at right angles to the abdomen when resting and look much

Burnet Companion (above) favours chalk and is found widely on the North Downs a couple of kilometres away

Common Carpet (right) on Heather

Privet Tortrix (below right) on Box. Larvae feed on various plants in addition to Privet and apparently they prefer dead leaves

more delicate than they are, have been observed every so often perched on windows. Those that have come into the house when windows have been left open and lights on in warm weather are headed by the Swallow-tailed Moth, which uniquely among our moths has 'tails' on its wings, and the Large Tabby. The former settled on a couch in the dining room for the night in the mid-1990s and the latter was on my bedroom curtain in 2000. One also appeared in 2012.

Other entrants via the windows include Large Yellow Underwing, Square-spot Rustic, Willow Beauty, the pretty little pyralid moth *Endotricha flammealis* (that one's larvae often feed on Bird's-foot-trefoil) and a species that arrived in Britain in 1959, the Cypress Pug.

Pyralid moths are small and a number have long snouts. The Large Tabby (above) was found on a bedroom curtain after coming in overnight and a *Crambus lathoniellus* (above right) flew on to the lawn when disturbed. *Crambus* moths have a distinct appearance – long and thin – but they are not easy to tell apart. The Small Magpie (right) is one of the brighter pyralids

As the name suggests, Common Nettle-tap uses Stinging Nettles as the food plant for its caterpillars

Willow Beauty is an almost guaranteed entrant if a window is left open with the light on

Pyrausta purpuralis, a colourful little day-flying pyralid moth, appears virtually every year, often on Heather

The last-named has profited from all the Cypress trees of one sort or another that have been planted in gardens over the last half-century. Reverting for a moment to the Swallow-tailed Moth, Ivy is the preferred food plant but they also use Horse-chestnut among other trees, and the latter acts as host to the Horse-chestnut Leaf Miner, which has had a huge visual effect since arriving in Britain at the start of this century. They can infest trees on a monumental scale, with up to 700 leaf mines possible on a single leaf. The leaves shrivel and turn brown, making the tree look very unsightly, but the damage seemingly does no harm because it occurs relatively late in the growing season.

In similar vein, a small moth with an inelegant English name, the Apple-leaf Skeletonizer, is not a miner but in places is regarded as a pest. Covered by a flimsy web, larvae eat the upper surface of leaves of Crab-apple principally but also cultivated Apple trees among others. This leads to the skeleton look that generated the name. There are not that many records in Surrey; one turned up on my Canadian Goldenrod in September 2012.

Silver Y basking on a log. The mark on the wing is often more ivory in colour than silver but overall the camouflage is effective

SPECIES OF BUTTERFLY RECORDED

Brimstone *Gonepteryx rhamni*
Brown Hairstreak *Thecla betulae*
Comma *Polygonia c-album*
Common Blue *Polyommatus icarus*
Dark Green Fritillary *Argynnis aglaja*
Gatekeeper *Pyronia tithonus*
Green-veined White *Artogeia napi*
Holly Blue *Celastrina argiolus*
Large Skipper *Ochlodes venatus*
Large White *Pieris brassicae*
Meadow Brown *Maniola jurtina*
Orange Tip *Anthocharis cardamines*

Painted Lady *Vanessa cardui*
Peacock *Inachis io*
Purple Hairstreak *Quercusia quercus*
Red Admiral *Vanessa atalanta*
Silver-washed Fritillary *Argynnis paphia*
Small Copper *Lycaena phlaeas* ab. *caeruleopunctata*
Small Skipper *Thymelicus sylvestris*
Small Tortoiseshell *Aglais urticae*
Small White *Artogeia rapae*
Speckled Wood *Pararge aegeria*

The Square-spot Rustic is a late summer species whose caterpillars feed mostly on grasses through the winter

SPECIES OF MOTH RECORDED

Angle Shades *Phlogophora meticulosa*
Apple-leaf Skeletonizer *Choreutis pariana*
Burnet Companion *Euclidia glyphica*
Cinnabar *Tyria jacobaeae*
Common Carpet *Epirrhoe alternata*
Common Nettle-tap *Anthophila fabriciana*
Cypress Pug *Eupithecia phoeniceata*
Dot *Melanchra persicariae*
Eyed Hawk-moth *Smerinthus ocellata*
Horse-chestnut Leaf Miner *Cameraria ohridella*
Large Tabby *Aglossa pinguinalis*
Large Yellow Underwing *Noctua pronuba*
Lime Hawk-moth *Mimas tiliae*
Orange Swift *Hepialus sylvina*
Plume moth prob. *Emmelina monodactyla*
Privet Tortrix *Clepsis consimilana*

Pyralid moth *Endotricha flammealis*
Pyralid moth *Pyrausta aurata*
Pyralid moth *Pyrausta purpuralis*
Red-belted Clearwing *Synanthedon myopaeformis*
Silver Y *Autographa gamma*
Small Magpie *Eurrhypara hortulata*
Snout moth *Crambus lathoniellus*
Square-spot Rustic *Xestia xanthographa*
Swallow-tailed Moth *Ourapteryx sambucaria*
Sycamore *Acronicta aceris*
White Ermine *Spilosoma lubricipeda*
Willow Beauty *Peribatodes rhomboidaria*
Yellow-legged Clearwing *Synanthedon vespiformis*
Yellow Shell *Camptogramma bilineata*

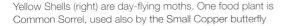

Sycamore adults (above) are nothing like so colourful as the caterpillars, a common arrangement with moths. They use Horse-chestnut as well as Sycamore for feeding

Yellow Shells (right) are day-flying moths. One food plant is Common Sorrel, used also by the Small Copper butterfly

Chapter 6
Bees

Bees are not only beautiful – they are also essential and one of the best indicators of how successful a wildlife-friendly gardener is. In Britain there are many more species of bee than is generally realised. The large social ones, bumblebees and honeybees, are those which tend to get noticed as they flit from flower to flower taking nectar or gathering pollen. Yet they represent not much more than ten per cent of the total bee fauna on the British mainland, which consists of around 250 species, some as small as five millimetres in length. Two hundred and twenty-two of them have been found in Surrey.

The work that bees, particularly but not exclusively honeybees and bumblebees, do in pollinating flowers and crops is well documented. They are made for the job, even to the point of generating an electrostatic charge in flight which assists them when it comes to collecting pollen. By some calculations, a bee is up to ten times more efficient gathering pollen by design than an invertebrate such as a butterfly or hoverfly is by accident. Crucially, 80 per cent of the different types of the world's flowering food crops, notably fruit, vegetables and nuts (though not grain), are pollinated by bees of one sort or another. Individually, honeybees are less efficient at pollinating than bumblebees or a number of solitary bees. In fact the role of solitary bees may be widely underestimated since social bees collect and transport a solid mixture of pollen and nectar, whereas nearly all solitary bees carry dry pollen. This simplifies the transfer of grains from one plant's anther to another's stigma.

Colletes succinctus male searching for females visiting Heather, the only plant used for collecting pollen to stock the nest

But they are solitary, and the honeybee's greatest strength (besides making a marvellous commercial crop in honey) is numerical. One hive can contain 10,000 workers while the largest bumblebee nest will not hold much more than 300. Surrey has a considerable number of hives, and membership of the local beekeepers' association has been increasing recently. In so far as the county has never been a stronghold of arable farming, there must be a suspicion that a welcome and progressive boost in suitable flora grown in gardens has benefited honeybees as well as other bees.

Honeybees cannot do everything though; bumblebees are essential for pollinating certain plants since they have a 'buzz pollination' technique not available to honeybees, whereby they rapidly vibrate flowers. This means that commercially or in the garden such crops as tomatoes, cucumbers, runner beans, broad beans and soft fruits including raspberries need bumblebees if they are not to be pollinated manually. Hand pollination is used regularly with tomatoes grown in large greenhouses, with melons and with dates to give three examples, but it simply is not practicable with most crops. In the garden or the allotment the natural way is the best way.

Bumblebees also make a major contribution to the pollination of our wildflowers, and the disappearance of so many flower meadows in Britain over the last 60 years undoubtedly has disadvantaged them. Changes in farming practices leading to insufficient protracted foraging opportunities are just one in a suite of difficulties bees have been facing in recent decades. Others are the arrival of the Varroa mite with honeybees and too casual use of pesticides. A National Environment Research Council report published in 2010 noted that the economic value of bees to British crops by pollination was up to £440 million per annum, equivalent to 13 per cent of farming income. It added that in the previous two years the number of honeybees had fallen by between ten and 15 per cent. The poor summer of 2012 was unhelpful too, with a 72

Epeolus cruciger, a cuckoo bee of *Colletes succinctus* that has been seen only once in the garden

One of a dozen *Colletes hederae* males that took nectar from Canadian Goldenrod in September-October 2012

Hylaeus communis female nears her nest in a brick. This is the most successful of the yellow-faced bees

Male *Hylaeus pictipes*, a scarce species with distinctive black kidney-shaped marks on the legs

Male *Hylaeus signatus* on Wild Mignonette, showing the extensive pale markings on the face that are more typical of males of the genus than females

per cent drop in honey production in Britain.

In the last 75 years two British species of bumblebee have become extinct and 15 of the remaining 23 have undergone a contraction in range. In Surrey three species have become extinct since 1900 and four others are giving cause for concern. A report in the Journal of Insect Conservation in 2011 using evidence provided by 'citizen scientists' claimed that one of our commonest bumblebees, the Common Carder Bee *Bombus pascuorum*, has undergone a fall of around 50 per cent in numbers nationally in the last 20 years. My observations in the garden, in Surrey generally and in north-west England do not support the belief that such a drastic collapse has occurred with this species but for bumblebees overall many of the signs are not encouraging.

The biggest plus is the arrival of a new species, the Tree Bumblebee *Bombus hypnorum*, which reached us from continental Europe in 2001 and is extending its range rapidly.

Large-scale actions are essential to help the species that are in trouble though. Among these, Operation Pollinator, sponsored by Syngenta, is an international five-year biodiversity programme to boost the number of pollinating insects on commercial farms, by creating specific habitats tailored to local conditions and native insects. Also, reasonably large areas in Kent were made much more bee-friendly in the run-up to the reintroduction of the formerly extinct Short-haired Bumblebee *Bombus subterraneus* at Dungeness in 2012.

Work on a smaller scale can assist too. Little patches of wildflowers in field corners and margins, on waste ground, on roadside verges and on motorway embankments are invaluable, and gardeners can play a big part as well. Since 2005 in my garden honeybees, 11 types of bumblebee led by *Bombus lapidarius*, *Bombus pascuorum*, *Bombus pratorum* and lately *Bombus hypnorum*, and 70 species of solitary bee have been logged. Many of these, including bumblebees, can be decidedly difficult to identify to species and I am grateful to David Baldock, author of *Bees of Surrey* and *Wasps of Surrey*, for assisting and encouraging me in this area as well as with wasps.

The overall tally of 82 bees compares with 59 identified in Dr Owen's garden in Leicester, but that merely reflects the difference in number of species in the two counties. Leicestershire has had fewer than 100 types of bee recorded. Principally, the bees noted in my garden have been visiting such nectar- and pollen-rich plants as Cotoneaster, Escallonia, Firethorn, Heather, Hebe, Lavender and yellow *Asteraceae*. Twenty-five of the total seen are nationally rare or scarce, or have been found in less than ten per cent of the 550 two-kilometre squares (tetrads) used for recording in Surrey. That is satisfying, especially as Surrey has one of the most complete invertebrate recording schemes in Britain.

It is worth pointing out here that even if a gardener keen on wildlife fails to see much activity on flowers that he or she has planted

A female *Nomada signata* cuckoo bee landing by a burrow being used for nesting by the host, *Andrena fulva*. This scarce species was present in the garden for several years up to 2008

specifically to attract invertebrates, such a snapshot is highly unlikely to be representative. One would need to watch flowers for hour after hour and day after day to obtain an accurate picture of their usage. As a sidelight on this, in the spring of 2012, despite being hampered by dismal weather at times, I kept a much closer eye on my flowers than previously and found one cuckoo bee and four solitary mining bee species new to the garden. All five, plus another newcomer in the summer, had been recorded from nearby sites in recent years, confirming just how local the personnel tend to be. As a rule, they 'drop in' for a particular reason, be it to nest, find pollen, take nectar or, in the case of cuckoo bees, locate a host. An exception was a single example of the mining bee *Andrena argentata*. This bee is present at Reigate Heath, a Site of Special Scientific Interest a couple of kilometres away, but has not been found within closer reach of the garden. Anyway, the new cuckoo bee mentioned above was *Nomada striata* and the five new miners were *Andrena flavipes*, the distinctly hairy and dashingly coloured *Andrena nigroaenea*, and three tiny bees measuring only six millimetres, *Andrena minutula*, *Lasioglossum minutissimum* and *Lasioglossum smeathmanellum*.

Putting in plants that have pollen and

Freshly-emerged female *Andrena fulva*, with her bright orange livery rather giving the lie to the colloquial name Tawny Mining Bee

Female *Andrena nigroaenea*, one of the largest of the genus, taking nectar from Garden Star-of-Bethlehem in the front border

Male *Andrena labialis*, with brighter facial markings than most male mining bees. This species is an irregular visitor

nectar through the year for bees, as detailed in Chapter 1, is not the whole story though. Accommodation is equally important yet sadly this is where many gardeners probably would draw the line. Rougher margins with bare patches of earth used for nesting, sometimes by bumblebees and invariably by such solitary bees as the Tawny Mining Bee *Andrena fulva*, could be seen as making a smart garden untidy but they provide a valuable habitat. *Andrena fulva* and the rare cuckoo bee that uses it as host, *Nomada signata*, were present in the top lawn from 2005 to 2008 but oddly, despite no alterations being made to the habitat, there has

Male *Halictus rubicundus* having a systematic clean-up

been no breeding since. This is a confident statement because *Andrena fulva* nests are always quite conspicuous due to the small mound of soil around them. As with other fossorial or aerial nesters, the excavation and spoil removal are effected by a splendid combination of mandibles and legs. (The scientific term for *Nomada signata*, and all other solitary cuckoo bees and cuckoo wasps, is cleptoparasite, defined as a species whose progeny scavenge eggs or larvae, plus the pollen or prey provided for them, in the nest of another species.)

Bare patches of earth are not the only valuable habitat for invertebrates that many people would view as unacceptable. The same often goes for good-sized pieces of dead wood gathered together, but these represent an outstanding breeding location for certain bees, wasps and beetles – old beetle holes are a regular haunt for a number of species. To my eyes, a pile of bleaching wood is far from unattractive, boasting an appealing sculptural aspect. Many more gardens could host such a pile, providing the wood was of the right type – the best trees are Beech and Willow while some, such as False-acacia, are completely

Female *Lasioglossum morio*, a small and common bee showing the bronzy sheen several of the genus have

Male *Anthophora bimaculata*. Green eyes are distinctive of the species, which is a noisy flier and makes only sporadic appearances in the garden

inappropriate because decay takes place incredibly slowly. The wood also needs replenishing every so often since the logs that draw in bees and wasps most readily frequently appear to be not too many years off total collapse.

Artificial assistance can also be provided without too much trouble, and wooden or plastic insect boxes, often called 'bee hotels', are by no means 'untidy'. Placed in a reasonably sunny position, such as on a fence post, shed or the wall of a property, they can contain bamboo canes, cardboard tubes, drilled bricks, drilled wood and any hollow or pithy stem such as reed or bramble. One point to remember is that the boxes do need to be secure against such problems as excessive wind and rain or prowling mammals. Purpose-built boxes are available widely for sale and may also be constructed relatively easily at home from available materials. They are definitely increasing in popularity and it would be fascinating to know how much activity their purchasers see in them each year.

For a naturalist, one of the great things about bees, and wasps even more, is that unlike so many invertebrates they have fascinating behaviour which, given a degree of patience, can be observed relatively easily. There is also a chance of discovering something new, since their lives have not received anything like the intensive study devoted to birds and mammals. With no

concerns from me or my mother about maintaining an artificial tidiness, in 2007 and 2008 I set up two sections of standing dead wood near the greenhouse towards the top of the garden, and in 2009 several insect boxes were added. The wood was mostly Beech. Greatly to my pleasure, all these brought results, with the predictable consequence that further boxes were added in 2010 and 2011, some made by me plus three kindly provided by Robin Dean of the Red Beehive Company and one by Dr Adam Bates of the University of Birmingham.

By 2012 potentially there was a huge amount of activity to observe and enjoy thanks to the insertion in the ground of half a double bed containing five boxes, 14 short logs drilled with holes ranging in size from two millimetres to 12 millimetres, and several standing pieces of dead wood. The notion that the boxes were doing a lot of good and presenting a chance for detailed scientific study to ascertain more about the species

Anthophora plumipes female showing the red pollen-gathering hairs which contrast finely with the black body

Male *Melecta albifrons*, a large and quite scarce cuckoo bee that targets *Anthophora plumipes*

involved was pleasing. Moreover, there is no denying that on a sunny day watching animals in frantic activity is rather relaxing, even if in this instance the relaxation tends to be interrupted by strenuous attempts to obtain good photographs of them. The shame was that the summer of 2012 brought so few sunny days.

The bee species which have utilised the opportunities offered in recent years – the wasps are dealt with in the next chapter – are led by the Red Mason Bee *Osmia bicornis*, formerly *Osmia rufa*, which completed eight nests in 2010, then 35 nests in bamboo, brick and cardboard tubes between April and June 2011. Once you have a colony of this handsome species it is likely to grow and grow, without having a damaging effect on the amount of pollen available for other species. The only damaging effect can be on soft mortar in walls if a large number nest annually in a house, a factor sometimes in the Cotswolds but rarely if ever in Surrey.

With all the rain in April and early May 2012 female Red Mason Bees were not evident until mid-May, after males had been noticed six weeks earlier. They soon made up for lost time though and there was a mating frenzy,

Male Blue Carpenter Bee *Ceratina cyanea* on dead bramble, the usual location for nests

Melitta haemorrhoidalis males, showing how markedly they can bleach in just three weeks after emergence. Males had been spotted in the Canterbury-bells in 2010 and were back in 2012 when two females who collected pollen from around 40 plants were the first known to have bred in this part of Surrey for more than half a century. Males bustle into flower heads in pursuit of females, even those which are gathering pollen and hence are unavailable for mating (below)

Red Mason Bees *Osmia bicornis* mating in May 2012, with two males trying their luck. Females gather pollen busily to stock cells then (opposite) collect soil which they moisten to seal the cells inside the nest and the nest itself. The drilled brick in the box made by Schwegler is the most popular location

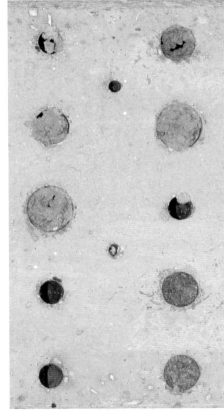

This *Osmia leaiana* female attempted three nests in 2012 but two of them appeared to be broken into. Pollen is gathered mainly from yellow Aster flowers and the cells and nest are closed with masticated leaves

The Blue Mason Bee *Osmia caerulescens* has nested every year in the purpose-built boxes, using bamboo, drilled brick or cut reeds. Pollen is gathered from various plants and, as with *Osmia leaiana*, cells are closed with masticated leaves

which I managed to catch on camera, with 52 nests being completed by the start of July. The containers used measured between four millimetres and 12 millimetres since the females were of varied size. One spurned the purpose-built opportunities presented and chose to nest in an old fence post, which needed altogether more work on her part. By far the most popular nesting site was the brick in one nest box manufactured in Germany, which had 18 completed nests from a total of 35 holes of suitable size available. Site loyalty probably is a consideration in this, since a bee may well return to the spot where she emerged and there had been 13 nests in the brick in 2011. Perhaps confirming this, three pieces of bamboo in another box that were used in 2011 were also used in 2012, apparently in preference to similar pieces in the box.

Red Mason Bees are strikingly attractive and make ubiquitous and exceptional pollinators, using many flowers including those of fruit trees, with the result that they have lately been used commercially for this purpose. They are among a minority of bee species that gather pollen using hairs underneath the abdomen – most, including bumblebees, use hairs on the hind legs. The five or six Red Mason Bee cells within a nest, each containing pollen and an egg, and the nest itself are closed with masticated soil. The soil used, as with all the local wasps in the boxes, is sand, and the fact that the resultant seal is so firm may be a testimony to the constitution of the saliva of the insects concerned.

Firm as these plugs in the ends of nests are, they are not strong enough to offer any defence against determined raiders. In 2011 most of the Red Mason Bee nests were attacked and the initial couple of cells opened, quite possibly by a Great-spotted Woodpecker. Other assailants may include Blue Tits and earwigs but their efforts are unlikely to compromise a colony seriously. To try and help the bees against the birds, 2012 saw me covering the nests in the brick with duck tape – which a woodpecker broke through late in the season – and putting chicken wire in front of the large wooden nesting structure.

Smaller bees to nest, as a rule also carrying pollen under the abdomen, included two species which use masticated leaves to close each cell and the nest, the Blue Mason Bee *Osmia caerulescens* and *Osmia leaiana*. In 2012 the latter used a hole drilled in a cut log for her first nest and sections of bamboo cane for her second and third. Two other bees to nest in these purpose-built structures were the yellow-faced bee *Hylaeus communis* and the nationally rare Daisy Carpenter Bee *Heriades truncorum* plus its scarce cuckoo bee *Stelis breviuscula*. *Hylaeus communis* – the genus carries pollen in the crop with nectar, rather than on the body – completed six nests in a brick and cut stems in 2011. Close observation showed that the species can have two broods, which was known in continental Europe but

Face-to-face courtship behaviour precedes mating for this pair of Daisy Carpenter Bees *Heriades truncorum*, though as so often they are besieged by another male (below). Opposite, pollen collection does not always go uninterrupted if fresh males have emerged and are looking for mates, as one female on Fleabane finds out. Pollen is carried under the abdomen and resin is ferried in the mandibles then used with artistry to make cell partitions and seal the nest

The number of nests Daisy Carpenter Bees complete each year can make life complicated, not least because follow-ups are often developed close to the original nest. Brief but lively territorial disputes between females, with mandibles bared, are commonplace

had not been confirmed previously in Britain though strongly suspected.

The Daisy Carpenter Bee is only seven or eight millimetres long and is a personal favourite. They look smashing, coloured black with white bands and bright orange hairs underneath to gather pollen, they work tremendously hard, with one female I logged gathering ten loads of pollen in just over half an hour, and they have fascinating behaviour. The exclusive source of pollen is yellow *Asteraceae* flowers, including such garden perennials as Heliopsis, Bidens, Sneezeweed and Canadian Goldenrod, plus Ragwort in the wild. Almost certainly the popularity of bright yellow flowers for gardeners in borders in the period June to September has presented this pretty species with an opportunity to boost its numbers and may give it a chance of spreading beyond the south-eastern stronghold. They were found in Norfolk in 2012. Daisy Carpenter Bees certainly are

thriving in Surrey. Besides pollen, what these bees need is resin to close each individual cell and the end of the nest, where the seal sets very hard, making life tough for any potential cuckoo bee, parasite or predator that arrives too late. Resin is often taken from pine trees and other conifers but deciduous trees can also be used and the bees are spoiled for choice around Reigate. Regrettably I have never seen a female gathering resin, which they manage to work very skilfully without getting covered in what is a distinctly sticky substance.

Daisy Carpenter Bees completed just two nests in cut reeds in 2010, managed 32 in the same box in 2011 and 38 in 2012 when they had a staggered emergence, between early July and mid-August. The diameter of each stem used for nesting was between two and a half and four millimetres, in other words pretty small. Intriguingly, while courtship behaviour is not commonly noticed with solitary bees – much of

Female cuckoo bee *Stelis breviuscula* checking a bee box containing nests of the host, the Daisy Carpenter Bee, and emerging from a stem covered in pollen

the mating looks to involve strong coercion – in 2012 the Daisy Carpenter Bees showed what can be done. A male waited outside a reed for a female to emerge, going in several times, and on three occasions over two days he and she engaged in what can be called a non-aggressive tête-à-tête. Immediately after the final get-together she came out and they mated.

One consequence of so much activity in a small area has been regular disputes, initially between males aiming to catch females to mate with, then between females, including when one went into another's nest by mistake. The error was understandable because orientation among some solitary bees is not brilliant, especially when all the nest entrances look so similar and there are a number close together. The arguments between females tended to be short but sharp and resulted in no visible injuries. This led me to wonder whether insect boxes by their very nature could be a mixed blessing, in so far as they may encourage

Megachile ligniseca is a large leaf-cutter bee and here a female is placing a piece of leaf in her nest in a drilled log. The artistry involved in the process is evident in the cross-section of part of another set of cells in a bamboo cane. Each neat parcel of leaves starts off containing pollen and an egg and finishes up holding the pupa awaiting emergence.

aggression, which would not necessarily be seen very frequently in the wild and might be unhelpful. One of the most interesting pieces of behaviour came in 2012 when two females spent an hour and a half closing one nest. They were not co-operating, there were some clashes, but neither would give up until the job had been finished. Perhaps one was suffering from a sort of senility, which seemingly may affect bees that are near the end of their working lives after weeks of endeavour, or perhaps both bees had stocked the one nest. The latter would be a very rare occurrence and certainly not typical for a solitary species.

Female *Megachile centuncularis* having a brief respite before taking her cut leaf back to a nest in brickwork, indicated by the reddish powder on her thorax

Any concentration of nests also seems to allow parasites, especially tiny wasps in late summer and early autumn, to focus their efforts more effectively than usual. Nearly all the *Hylaeus communis* nests in 2011 seemed to have been invaded, probably by parasitic wasps, but that had no overall effect on breeding capacity in 2012 when ten nests were completed. Two other 'cuckoos' that go for *Hylaeus* species and/or Daisy Carpenter Bees among others, laying eggs on larvae, are the bizarrely shaped, elongated *Gasteruption jaculator* and *Gasteruption assectator*. The former has a remarkably long ovipositor and two females spent much of July and August 2012 hovering in front of the cut reeds where they had abundant targets.

Other species which have nested in the garden, using soil like the Tawny Mining Bee, include the Red-tailed Bumblebee *Bombus lapidarius*, the Buff-tailed Bumblebee *Bombus terrestris*, the Common Carder Bee *Bombus pascuorum*, the Bryony Bee *Andrena florea* and three other mining bees, *Andrena dorsata*, *Andrena haemorrhoa* and *Andrena nitida*. Bumblebees anywhere can have trouble with

Coelioxys elongata is a cuckoo bee of leaf-cutter bees. Females of the genus have a distinctly pointed abdomen whereas males have a blunter tip with a series of prongs. They are pictured on Escallonia and Bidens

Female Wool Carder Bee *Anthidium manicatum*, with the yellow markings on the abdomen clearly visible. The hairier and more ferocious-looking male is shown on the opening pages of this chapter

Female *Stelis punctulatissima*, a cuckoo bee that uses *Anthidium manicatum* as host

The cuckoo bee *Sphecodes ephippius* and other members of the genus look more like solitary wasps than bees. This one is taking nectar from Wild Carrot

mammals, principally Badgers but also Red Foxes, digging out their nests. They also suffer from the attentions of cuckoo bumblebees such as *Bombus rupestris* and *Bombus vestalis*, females of which invade a nest, kill or usurp the resident queen and lay eggs which produce larvae that the old queen's worker offspring unknowingly rear as if they were from their own species.

The solitary bees do not face being dug out unless they have nested in the vegetable plot or borders but they do face attacks from cuckoo bees. Remarkably, getting on for a quarter of the British list of bees are cuckoo bees and many of them look much more like wasps, with markings that are black and red (*Sphecodes*) or mostly yellow and black (*Nomada*). Twenty-two of the bee species seen in the garden have been cuckoo bees and several of them are far from common, namely *Nomada signata*, *Stelis breviuscula* and *Stelis punctulatissima*.

Locally, the same goes for an *Epeolus cruciger*, a cuckoo bee using the Common Colletes *Colletes succinctus*, that I spotted on Heather in 2008. That remains the only sighting in this part of Surrey. Two other cuckoo bees, *Coelioxys inermis* and *Coelioxys elongata*, are not seen terribly frequently

across Britain, let alone Surrey. This pair uses leaf-cutter bees to breed from and four of that genus (*Megachile centuncularis*, *Megachile ligniseca*, *Megachile versicolor* and *Megachile willughbiella*) have been seen gathering pollen in the garden borders with two nesting. However, I have never had evidence of their cutting leaves from the favoured Rose bushes, or anything else for that matter.

Stelis punctulatissima, mentioned above, is a cuckoo bee that goes for the handsome Wool Carder Bee *Anthidium manicatum*. The latter species, which is drawn to the plant Lamb's Ears *Stachys byzantina* to gather nesting material from the leaves, has been in the garden only a couple of times, which is a pity given how marvellous they look. As an exception to the general rule among solitary bees, male *Anthidium manicatum* can be significantly bigger than females and patrol breeding territories aggressively. They are capable of killing other invertebrates entering

'Des res' for bees and wasps, with standing dead wood, drilled logs, bamboo canes, cardboard tubes and reeds

Female cuckoo bee *Nomada marshamella* looking for host mining bee nests in the rockery under the Heather

Nomada ruficornis, with a lot of orange-brown markings, is an annual visitor in spring

Tree Bumblebee *Bombus hypnorum* queen on Mahonia

Nomada striata, a new species for the garden in 2012

Red-tailed Bumblebee *Bombus lapidarius* worker heading for a nest in the ground near the greenhouse. Unfortunately the colony was plundered by mammals

Nomada fabriciana male, one of the reddish coloured members of the genus

the territory, though as with so many savage tales drawn from nature there is no evidence that this happens frequently.

Without much doubt other ground-nesting species, and some 'aerial' nesters, have set up home in the garden without my being able to find them. These include the regularly seen yellow-faced bee *Hylaeus hyalinatus*, the lovely and nationally rare Blue Carpenter Bee *Ceratina cyanea*, which nests mostly in bramble stems, and the nationally scarce mining bee *Andrena labiata*. The last-named goes to speedwells in the wild and has visited Garden Star-of-Bethlehem and Firethorn in my garden – in 2011 one kept coming to the last-named to gather pollen. Species which have possibly nested are the yellow-faced bee *Hylaeus signatus*, which appeared the first year I grew

Male Early Bumblebee *Bombus pratorum* on Cotoneaster, showing tremendous yellow markings

Dark form male cuckoo bee *Bombus campestris*

Bombus rupestris, a cuckoo of *Bombus lapidarius*, is a ringer for the host apart from having darker wings

its favoured plant Mignonette but not afterwards, and another from that genus, the nationally scarce *Hylaeus pictipes*, which I have twice seen on Wild Carrot.

Against that, some visitors definitely do not nest in the garden. Among these are *Colletes succinctus* mentioned above, which takes pollen only from Heather but needs open sandy places in which to nest, and the Ivy Bee *Colletes hederae*, which takes pollen only from the plant after which it is named. This species arrived in mainland Britain in 2001 and is expanding its range rapidly; the first sighting in Surrey was by me in 2007 in the disused sandpit over the road from the house. The species is now thriving there with dozens of nests completed each year. Males have taken nectar in the garden many times, including

Cuckoo bee *Bombus vestalis* taking nectar from Hebe

Honeybee workers are ubiquitous in gathering pollen from as early as February to October. These two are using Crocuses and Canadian Goldenrod

SPECIES OF SOCIAL BEE RECORDED

Buff-tailed Bumblebee *Bombus terrestris*
Common Carder Bee *Bombus pascuorum*
Cuckoo bumblebee *Bombus campestris*
Cuckoo bumblebee *Bombus rupestris*
Cuckoo bumblebee *Bombus sylvestris*
Cuckoo bumblebee *Bombus vestalis*
Early Bumblebee *Bombus pratorum*
Garden Bumblebee *Bombus hortorum*
Honeybee *Apis mellifera*
Tree Bumblebee *Bombus hypnorum*
Red-tailed Bumblebee
Bombus lapidarius
White-tailed Bumblebee
Bombus lucorum

from some of the plentiful Ivy, and happily a female finally turned up to collect pollen in October 2012. Other non-nesters in the garden that use open sand locally include the striking *Anthophora bimaculata*, with gorgeous green eyes, and the Hairy-footed Flower Bee *Anthophora plumipes*. Like the Red Mason Bee, the latter can take advantage of walls with soft mortar. Its cuckoo bee *Melecta albifrons* has also visited the garden.

SPECIES OF SOLITARY BEE RECORDED

Andrena argentata	Halictus tumulorum
Andrena barbilabris	Heriades truncorum
Andrena bicolor	Hoplitis claviventris
Andrena dorsata	Hylaeus communis
Andrena flavipes	Hylaeus dilatatus
Andrena florea	Hylaeus hyalinatus
Andrena fulva	Hylaeus pictipes
Andrena fuscipes	Hylaeus signatus
Andrena haemorrhoa	Lasioglossum calceatum
Andrena labialis	Lasioglossum fulvicorne
Andrena labiata	Lasioglossum lativentre
Andrena minutula	Lasioglossum minutissimum
Andrena nigroaenea	Lasioglossum morio
Andrena nitida	Lasioglossum parvulum
Andrena semilaevis	Lasioglossum punctatissimum
Andrena trimmerana	Lasioglossum smeathmanellum
Anthidium manicatum	Lasioglossum villosulum
Anthophora furcata	Megachile centuncularis
Anthophora bimaculata	Megachile ligniseca
Anthophora plumipes	Megachile versicolor
Ceratina cyanea	Megachile willughbiella
Chelostoma campanularum	Melitta haemorrhoidalis
Chelostoma florisomne	Osmia bicornis (ex rufa)
Colletes hederae	Osmia caerulescens
Colletes succinctus	Osmia leaiana
Halictus rubicundus	Panurgus calcaratus

SPECIES OF CUCKOO BEE RECORDED

Coelioxys elongata	Nomada marshamella
Coelioxys inermis	Nomada panzeri
Epeolus cruciger	Nomada ruficornis
Melecta albifrons	Nomada signata
Nomada fabriciana	Nomada striata
Nomada flava	Sphecodes ephippius
Nomada flavoguttata	Sphecodes monilicornis
Nomada goodeniana	Stelis breviuscula
Nomada lathburiana	Stelis punctulatissima

Chapter 7
Wasps

Bees consistently receive a good press but the reverse is the case for wasps, based almost entirely on the activities of the social varieties. They cause trouble at picnics, they nest in your shrubbery, trees or roofs, they get woozy and hide invisibly when drunk from fruit or when cold, they come into any and every room in the house, but mainly – they sting. With the *Vespula* species in particular, that is the Common Wasp *Vespula vulgaris* and the German Wasp *Vespula germanica*, this can result in potentially fatal anaphylactic shock for a small proportion of people.

None of this is disputable, and it would be an exceptional, or exceptionally tolerant, naturalist who had never knocked seven bells out of a wasp which stung him or her, or removed a nest from close to their living quarters. But demonising social wasps for doing what comes naturally is a bit daft, especially when the demonisation is not entirely accurate. Generally, wasps in Europe sting defensively to protect themselves if attacked or seriously disturbed, with direct, unprovoked attacks uncommon. Moreover, the fact that social wasps are prolific at reducing pest species, especially flies, ought to make them popular with gardeners. With thousands of cells containing hungry larvae in a Common Wasp nest, a lot of flies need taking. Social wasps also pollinate some plants when taking nectar, and generations ago their fascinating, intricate and delicate method of nest construction by using wood fibres might just have inspired mankind to produce paper from wood pulp.

A Hornet worker on a favoured plant, Ivy. At 25 millimetres or more they are the largest of the social wasps

Apart from anything else, just as public perception of bees is based on the activities of a small proportion of species, namely the honeybee and bumblebees, so views of wasps rely almost entirely on a mere ten species out of a total of nearly 300 that have been recorded on the British mainland. Two hundred and forty-two of these have been seen in Surrey. They have varied and sometimes brilliant colouring, astonishing life cycles, a size ranging from two millimetres to 30 millimetres, and the ability to catch almost any kind of invertebrate from tiny thrip flies and aphids, up to shieldbugs, weevils, caterpillars, spiders and grasshoppers. They are remarkable creatures, by far my favourite family of invertebrates, and they certainly merit much more tolerance and support from homeowners and gardeners, given their ability to remove species seen as pests, especially aphids. I am proud to have created a habitat in the garden that saw 77 species of wasp turn up between 2005 and 2012, with at least 28 nesting. Even better, a higher proportion than with the bees – almost half – are nationally rare or scarce, or have been found in less than ten per cent of the two-kilometre squares used for recording in Surrey.

Common Wasp worker gathering wood to help develop a nest from pulp, and the early stages of a nest showing the delicacy of construction

The most spectacular and largest wasp is the Hornet, with queens measuring up to 30 millimetres. They are reasonably common in south-east England and although there is a close association with ancient deciduous woodland, Hornets are found fairly frequently in urban settings. Nests – in trees, underground or in buildings – can be massive, containing up to 1,500 cells which are re-used. As with other social wasps, prey consists mainly of flies but other social wasps, honeybees, moths, butterflies and spiders, even large Garden Spiders, are also taken. Hornets have not nested in the garden to my knowledge but they hunted prey there in 2010 and 2011, with Ivy blossom particularly favoured. Interestingly, they are not inconvenienced by cloudy conditions or even light rain and can hunt on bright nights too. Despite public perception to the contrary,

German Wasps getting inebriated by accident on a windfall Worcester Pearmain apple

Hornets are not aggressive, and give humans no trouble unless threatened. If you deliberately 'stir up a Hornets' nest' you get precisely what you deserve.

Among the other social wasps, Common Wasps try nesting in the house most years, with all the associated irritation on occasions. They can often be seen gathering wood for nesting from the garden fence or the dead wood placed up the garden for other species. Persistent visiting by social wasps to dead wood can be off-putting for the smaller species nesting there. Three other species are regular in the garden, but I have not found any nests – the most impressive is the Median Wasp

Saxon Wasp worker, a species of social wasp which is present most years but never numerous

Median Wasp male and dark-coloured worker. The male had landed in a glass of beer on a picnic table up the garden. This is a large species and workers vary in colouring, with many having much more yellow than this one

Chrysis ignita is the commonest cuckoo wasp in the garden. This female is exiting a host nest

Chrysis illigeri turned up in a plastic bowl with water. After being dried and photographed she was let go

The ruby-tail wasp *Pseudomalus auratus*, only six millimetres long, used to be an annual visitor seen on dead wood

Sexual dimorphism in colour is evident with the largest cuckoo wasp in the garden, *Hedychrum niemelai*, which takes nectar from Wild Carrot and Yarrow. Males have a mostly blue thorax while females show green and red

Dolichovespula media, which measures 20 millimetres or so and often nests in hedges. Their workers can be very dark in colour.

Moving on to solitary wasps, they are a tremendously dashing collection, none more so than the chrysids, usually known as ruby-tails or jewel wasps. These are fairly small cuckoo wasps using other often much larger species as hosts for their progeny. They are able to achieve this by stealth and by having armoured abdomens that enable them to curl into a ball and render futile any assault by a host returning to a nest while they are at work. Most people probably would have no idea ruby-tails exist, and if spotting one might not even think it was a wasp due to the exotic colouring. With the light refracting off their metallic coats it is sometimes tricky to know exactly what hue they are, but the variations usually involve beautiful reds, blues and greens.

A classic example is *Hedychrum niemelai*, a chunky species which targets nests of *Cerceris* digger wasps. Females are tri-coloured and males show just red and blue. Although formerly pretty rare, *Hedychrum niemelai* is becoming increasingly common in the south-east. They particularly like Yarrow and Wild Carrot for nectar, as does *Hedychridium roseum*, a cuckoo wasp of the digger wasp *Astata boops*. Neither of the cuckoos just mentioned breeds in the garden since their hosts are based in much more open sandy areas nearby. But one of the commonest

Tiphia femorata female (right) taking nectar from Wild Carrot, a plant they love. The characteristic red legs and hirsute aspect are evident

Trichrysis cyanea (below) is an entirely blue-green cuckoo wasp, so the term ruby-tail is hardly accurate here

Female *Sapyga quinquepunctata*, revealing the superior colour combination of red, black and white, and male with no red at all

ruby-tails does breed. The species is *Chrysis ignita*, which has a red abdomen and blue-green thorax, though the fact that there are several very similar species under the *Chrysis ignita* heading can complicate matters. They use mainly mason wasps as hosts, affording good views at the insect boxes in the garden with nests of *Ancistrocerus nigricornis* and *Ancistrocerus trifasciatus* (those two species are dealt with a little later in this chapter). I have watched two females waiting patiently for a quarter of an hour or so for an unwitting host to vacate its nest to go hunting; the

cuckoo then entered the tube to lay an egg. *Chrysis ignita* clearly is adaptable – a pupa in the nest of *Ancistrocerus nigricornis* needs to emerge in July along with the host's progeny, then probably mate and, if a female, overwinter. On the other hand a pupa in an *Ancistrocerus trifasciatus* nest can wait until the following spring when that host's offspring emerge. Their ability to work out how much time is available for development is little short of miraculous.

One scarce ruby-tail to turn up was *Chrysis illigeri*, which targets a digger wasp not yet

Spider-hunting wasp *Agenioideus cinctellus*, a small species, on the way to her nest in dead wood with a *Heliophanus* spider

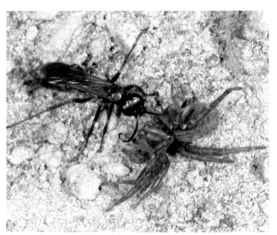

Anoplius nigerrimus (with prey) and *Anoplius infuscatus* are from the same genus but differ in colour and frequency since *Anoplius nigerrimus* is plentiful each year whereas *Anoplius infuscatus* appeared for the first time in 2012 when taking nectar from Wild Carrot

seen in the garden, the grasshopper catcher *Tachysphex pompiliformis*. In contrast, *Trichrysis cyanea* used to be common. They have no red colouring at all and use a variety of wood-nesting species as hosts including some bees. Ruby-tails like taking nectar from flowers but most of those found in the garden have usually been seen in action looking for potential host nests. For no apparent reason two species which used to be seen several times each year, *Trichrysis cyanea* and *Pseudomalus auratus*, have not been spotted since 2009. Potential hosts are still present in logs and such like, and probably even more numerous than formerly, so this shortfall is mysterious.

Arachnospila anceps is one of the spider-hunting wasps that store prey on vegetation while they prepare the nest in soil

Regular wood-nesting spider-hunting wasps include *Dipogon variegatus* (right) and *Auplopus carbonarius*. The former always catches one type of crab spider, *Xysticus cristatus*, and the strength of her mandibles and neck muscles must be prodigious to enable transportation. *Auplopus carbonarius* (below), which broke new ground by using a bamboo cane for nesting in 2012, often flies with prey having amputated most of the legs

One of the most attractive wasps of all is also a cuckoo but from a different family that uses only bees as hosts. This is *Sapyga quinquepunctata*, one of the so-called club-horned wasps and a species with striking red, black and white markings in the female – the male's face and antennae, shown at the start of this chapter, are exceptional. The Red Mason Bee *Osmia bicornis* is a regular host and I have watched several female *Sapyga quinquepunctata* going rapidly from one tube or hole to another to check whether there is an active nest. The easiest way to spot them, though, is when they are taking nectar, which again is done very speedily with a lot of flitting from flower head to flower head. Forget-Me-Nots and Sheep's-bit are both popular for this.

Spider-hunting wasps are incessantly active, with the result that they have been called jocularly '*Hymenoptera neurotica*.' They stock their nests with paralysed spiders for their young to feed on and although they have a shortage of colour, with black and red dominant, their behaviour is fascinating. They are in fact my favourite family of wasps. Thirteen species, a third of the British list, have

Although mason wasps including *Ancistrocerus nigricornis* and, with fewer yellow bands on the abdomen, *Ancistrocerus trifasciatus*, can and do use mortar in walls, installing insect boxes has assisted them. Both species catch micro-moth caterpillars, chiefly on trees, and flying back can involve tricky aerobatics if the prey is larger than the wasp, as with the green one pictured. The cells and end of each nest are sealed with moistened soil, which is gathered in the mandibles

The faces of male mason wasps are often rather yellow, as with this male *Ancistrocerus nigricornis*

Symmorphus bifasciatus made full use of the garden in 2011 when a female stocked a decayed elder stem with prey and took soil from a ransacked Red Mason Bee nest in a drilled brick to seal the cells in her own nest

turned up in the garden with nine confirmed to have nested. The ability of a wasp to subdue a spider, none of which are short on armament and some of which are larger than the wasp catching them, came as a surprise to me when I started studying Hymenoptera. But they are more mobile than the prey, have long legs and possess powerful stings, with the result that they do not often miss the target or allow a spider to get the upper hand.

Spiders seem to know when these wasps are on the prowl – I saw a fairly large one moving like lightning on the rockery when an *Auplopus carbonarius* was hunting. (English names are virtually non-existent for these wasps, perhaps in part because so many of them look exactly the same unless they are put under a microscope.) *Agenioideus cinctellus*, *Anoplius nigerrimus*, *Auplopus carbonarius*, *Dipogon subintermedius* and *Dipogon variegatus* have nested in my dead wood and *Anoplius nigerrimus* again, *Arachnospila anceps*, *Arachnospila trivialis* and *Priocnemis parvula* have nested in the soil, including in borders

Gymnomerus laevipes, a mason wasp that catches weevil larvae and nests in plant stems, is an occasional visitor. It seems to be declining nationally

and once in a regular bonfire site. *Auplopus carbonarius* is uncommon in flying with prey and unique in constructing collective cells of mud for its larvae. One broke new ground by using a bamboo cane in one of my boxes for her nest in 2012, and catching spiders I had not even seen around the property before. All the other spider-hunting wasps normally create one nest for each spider caught. Wild

Inexplicably, males of the digger wasp *Argogorytes mystaceus* have remarkably long antennae. This one is taking nectar from Hebe

Crossocerus annulipes (above) is a hard-working little digger wasp and up to ten nests are completed most years. They excavate large amounts of dead wood to make a nest and can catch up to 18 bugs an hour

Crossocerus megacephalus (left) returning to her nest in drilled wood with a *Pachygaster leachii* soldierfly

Crabro peltarius (below left) hunts flies and breeds in the nearby sandpit. Females visited in 2011 and 2012

Carrot is a great plant for attracting this family; I have had two new species for the garden taking nectar from this umbellifer, *Priocnemis exaltata* in 2011 and the black and orange *Anoplius infuscatus* in 2012.

Another species which catches spiders but comes from a different family is the skinny and elongated *Trypoxylon clavicerum*, which seems to love the cut reeds in one of my boxes. They stock the nests with immature spiders and more than 30 were completed in 2011, but since they proved to be double-brooded, the first time this had been confirmed in Britain, it was impossible to be precise about the number. There were almost as many nests in 2012. As with the Daisy Carpenter Bee, the

The Mournful Wasp *Pemphredon lugubris* is a real help since their prey consists of aphids of all kinds. The novelty of some using bamboo canes rather than dead wood for nests has resulted in a bit of comical 'millinery'

proximity to each other of so many of one species can lead to disputes, and these are not always settled without destruction – one *Trypoxylon clavicerum* got at another's nest in 2011 and pulled out the tiny spiders stocking it, with an egg visible on one that was left dangling.

The other wasps to have nested in the garden, chiefly in substrates or containers that I have put in for them, are led by the potter and mason wasps mentioned earlier in connection with the jewel wasp *Chrysis ignita*. *Ancistrocerus nigricornis*, *Ancistrocerus trifasciatus* and *Symmorphus bifasciatus* are black and yellow and benefit aesthetically from the colouring being exceptionally rich. The life cycle of *Ancistrocerus nigricornis*, with its overwintering as an adult, is rare among British solitary wasps and gives the species a distinct edge if April and May are fine and warm. Against that, a succession of cool and

Psenulus pallipes (above) flying back to her nest in a reed with an aphid, one of around 200 used to stock the cells

This *Passaloecus corniger* female (left) with an aphid in her mandibles is about to enter her nest in wood in my main structure near the greenhouse. She has just stolen the prey from a solitary wasp nest in a nearby insect box

damp springs is no use for the species, which appears to have suffered a decline nationally in recent years. Both *Ancistrocerus trifasciatus* and *Symmorphus bifasciatus* are fully-grown pupae through the winter and emerge as adults in May or June. All three can utilise cardboard tubes or bamboo and the two *Ancistrocerus* species provided a lot of entertainment in 2011 when they completed 11 nests.

Their activities involved a massive amount of work since every nest had up to six cells, closed with masticated mud, each containing half a dozen micro-moth caterpillars. Much of the prey quite possibly was taken from Oak trees close by in the park and some days the *Ancistrocerus nigricornis* were catching six caterpillars in 40 minutes or less. Whatever the distance involved in foraging, the diligence and strength of the wasps in achieving such a

Gorytes laticinctus female, a particular favourite photographed after being taken in the gazebo

tally is little short of phenomenal since the caterpillars are carried under their bodies, creating wind resistance, and are subdued but not dead. In fact towards the end of the nesting period in May 2011 a few prey items were longer than the wasp, no doubt due to accelerated development after an uncommonly warm two months. Transporting these must have been distinctly problematic, not least because potentially, due to the slower flight, it laid the wasp more open than usual to predation by birds.

In 2012 the poor weather in April, May and June meant that only four *Ancistrocerus nigricornis* nests were completed in the tubes and bamboo. Another genuinely lived up to the description mason wasp by taking advantage of a hole in the mortar between bricks at the back of the kitchen. Sadly in 2012 there was no sign of *Symmorphus bifasciatus*, which differs from the two *Ancistrocerus* species in collecting beetle larvae as prey. Intriguingly this species engaged in a bit of banditry in 2011, when filching mud from a ransacked Red Mason Bee nest in a brick to use in her own nest ten metres away.

All the other species to have nested have been so-called digger wasps, though since most of them use wood the term is a bit imprecise. Indeed, not all of the wood-nesting species carry out extensive excavation, notably *Crossocerus megacephalus, Ectemnius cavifrons, Ectemnius continuus, Passaloecus corniger, Passaloecus gracilis, Rhopalum clavipes, Rhopalum coarctatum, Spilomena beata, Stigmus pendulus*

Female *Lestiphorus bicinctus*, another species that has turned up in the gazebo

Stigmus digger wasps are only a few millimetres long and nest in good numbers in dead wood in the garden. This female *Stigmus pendulus*, a species fairly new to Britain, has an aphid captured on a plant in the border

and *Stigmus solskyi.* Most of these use old beetle holes duly customised, as do *Mimumesa dahlbomi* and *Crossocerus annulipes,* the difference being that the latter pair can remove prodigious quantities of wood shavings. They catch bugs (Hemiptera), which brings home the benefits the majority of all these wasps can effect for a gardener.

The Mournful Wasp *Pemphredon lugubris* is the commonest breeder in the garden, with getting on for 20 nests completed in dead wood each year plus – seemingly a rarity in Britain – two completed in bamboo canes in

---

Nysson trimaculatus (left), a scarce cuckoo wasp of *Lestiphorus bicinctus*, has turned up several times

Spilomena beata (below) is minute, measuring only three millimetres and nesting in wood, catching a type of fly called a thrip or thunderfly. Males, as here, show a significant amount of yellow on the face

Female *Rhopalum clavipes* heading for her nest. Clearly shown are the long legs that assist in carrying varied prey, and the red marking which separates the species from virtually all other digger wasps nesting in wood

2011 and three in 2012. A Mournful Wasp may have six cells in her nest in a branched system, with up to 40 aphids of varying size in each. Do the maths and you can see how many of these bugs they are taking out of circulation. The same applies to the little black wasp *Psenulus pallipes*, which uses stems or wood and can catch a couple of hundred aphids to stock the six to eight cells in each nest. This species completed four nests in the garden in 2011 and five the year after.

The two *Passaloecus* species seen nesting also take aphids but *Passaloecus corniger* has a cunning and lazy ploy whereby it does not always bother catching them itself, preferring to rob other wasps, especially *Psenulus pallipes*. One female in 2012 spent much of her time patrolling the cut stems where *Psenulus pallipes* nested and definitely filched some aphids. The larger wood-nesting solitary wasps *Ectemnius cavifrons*, *Ectemnius cephalotes* and *Ectemnius continuus* have not bred consistently in recent years despite the provision of plenty of potential nest sites. (*Ectemnius cephalotes*, which sometimes nests gregariously, has not been seen since 2005.) All three catch flies including fair-sized hoverflies. The same goes for the ground-nesting *Mellinus arvensis*, which

Oxybelus uniglumis is a habitual nectar feeder through the summer but has not nested in the garden, preferring the nearby sandpit. This is a female and they catch small flies

Mating *Rhopalum coarctatum*, a new species for the garden in 2012. They are much blacker than *Rhopalum clavipes* but the legs show attractive colours

Their elongate appearance and the fact that they catch immature spiders make *Trypoxylon clavicerum* easy to distinguish from the other wasps nesting in the cut reeds. Males harry females mercilessly in the hope of mating

takes advantage of Red Fox dung and Ivy blossom to find its favoured prey and almost every year tries to create at least one burrow in the vegetable plot. There are numerous nests in the disused sandpit over the road and three females nested in a tiny bank by the greenhouse in 2012.

One of the most interesting wood nesters in 2011 was the little *Crossocerus megacephalus*, which catches flies, especially soldierflies. I had never noticed any soldierflies in the garden or the surrounding area but this female wasp caught at least two varieties. Unfortunately she died after completing one nest in a drilled wooden block and starting another.

Species which come to take nectar or hunt are led by the Beewolf *Philanthus triangulum*, which normally catches only honeybees and can have a serious effect on their numbers when there are large aggregations of nests as sometimes on the western Surrey heaths. They take nectar from Heather and Canadian Goldenrod in the garden, as does another

species which preys on smaller bees, *Cerceris rybyensis*, and one that catches weevils, *Cerceris arenaria*. Two species which visit almost every year are *Astata boops*, mentioned above in relation to the cuckoo wasp *Hedychridium roseum*, and *Tiphia femorata*. The latter, with splendid hairy red legs, is known as the Beetle-killing Wasp and is a parasitoid that burrows into the ground to lay eggs on the larvae of scarab beetles including chafers. Both these wasps are partial to Wild Carrot and there were three female *Tiphia femorata* and two males on this plant in August 2012. Parasitoid wasps differ from cuckoo wasps in

Ectemnius cavifrons does pretty well in decayed Beech logs some years, with three nests completed in 2010 and seven in 2012. The main prey is hoverflies, which are plentiful in the garden. Females leave nests even faster than they enter them (below)

having larvae that develop entirely on or in a living host, which is always killed in the end.

Other cuckoo wasps that arrive now and then are *Nysson spinosus* and *Nysson trimaculatus*, together with their hosts *Argogorytes mystaceus* (usually taking nectar from Hebe or Escallonia), *Lestiphorus bicinctus* and *Gorytes laticinctus*. I once rescued a *Nysson trimaculatus* from the water butt. The hosts, which catch spittle-bug nymphs or bugs, are black and yellow and extremely attractive, with fairly brightly coloured antennae and, in the case of the nationally rare but increasing *Gorytes laticinctus*, a handsome yellow face. This one and *Lestiphorus bicinctus* have both appeared inside the gazebo used for al fresco meals on the lawn. Indeed, that is the only place locally where I have seen *Gorytes laticinctus*, which turned up in July 2009, July 2010 and July 2012.

The gazebo is not large compared with many, measuring under two metres all round with a high point just over two metres above the ground, but the cotton cover, open on all sides, acts as a useful trap for all sorts of invertebrates that fly in although quite a high proportion escape relatively quickly. Forty-one species of wasp and 30 types of bee have 'visited', often leading to my leaping up

Ectemnius continuus female returning with prey to a nest from which she had evicted a Mournful Wasp in 2007

Ectemnius cephalotes (left) female carrying a bluebottle towards her nest in dead wood in 2005. *Cerceris arenaria* (above) catches weevils and is in the garden every year when the Canadian Goldenrod is in bloom

to try and put each in a plastic pot before using a loupe to try and check identification. As a result, lunch can be slightly episodic and cause amused surprise to any guests who have not been warned. Any uncommon species I am able to identify are brought into the house and placed in the fridge for a while to make photographing them easier. They are then released with no harm done. Ones that I am unable to identify – and some can be extremely difficult – are passed on to David Baldock.

The largest group of wasps are parasites, with more than 6,000 species identified so far in Britain, meaning they outnumber the aculeate (having a sting) Hymenoptera by a wide margin. Most are tiny and inconspicuous but the Ichneumonidae family can be sizeable, wonderfully coloured, often mimicking social wasps, and tend to have long antennae with several dozen segments in extreme instances. The larvae are carnivorous and develop in a huge range of

The Beewolf *Philanthus triangulum* is not popular since it catches honeybees, but the wasp's numbers are hardly large enough locally to be a problem. This female has more yellow on the abdomen than usual but clearly shows the diagnostic chestnut marking on the head

Mellinus arvensis is a species of late summer which catches a wide variety of flies to stock often deep nests dug in sand. Males can be vastly smaller than females, as a glance at the mating pair confirms. After flying with prey slung underneath following capture, the female always changes position and pulls the fly into the nest backwards

Ichneumon sarcitorius male, a large species with effective wasp mimicry in the colouring

Ichneumon suspiciosus is one of the bonniest of the family and is showing the colours superbly here

Listrodromus nycthemerus can have dramatic effects on populations of the Holly Blue butterfly

Cratichneumon species with the two-tone antennae seen in a number of ichneumons

host invertebrates but adults obtain their sustenance from such substances as nectar and honeydew.

The most striking visually and behaviourally are females with an ovipositor as long as the rest of the insect or longer. These devices, with all the penetration of a long hypodermic needle, are used with astonishing precision to insert eggs in the larvae or pupae of the host. The latter are located accurately by use of scent and sensory perception in the legs; the ichneumon then can take up to half an hour applying her ovipositor to penetrate the wood, find the larva and lay an egg on it. *Ephialtes manifestator*, measuring up to 60 millimetres including the ovipositor, preys on beetles while the smaller *Perithous scurra* parasitises various wood and stem-nesting solitary wasps, notably *Pemphredon* species. This one can be seen every year on the logs up the garden where *Pemphredon lugubris* and sometimes *Pemphredon morio* nest.

Perhaps the best known and certainly the

The Sabre Wasp *Rhyssa persuasoria* (above) is our largest ichneumon wasp though in length a female *Ephialtes manifestator* (left) is not too far behind

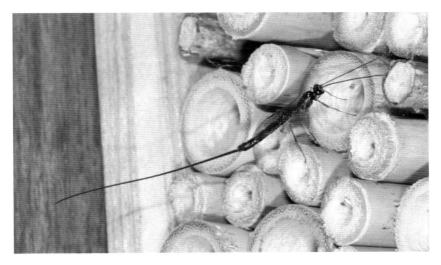

largest of the family in Britain is the Giant Ichneumon or Sabre Wasp, *Rhyssa persuasoria*, which can measure 80 millimetres from head to tip of ovipositor. The name translates as 'persuasive burglar' and eggs are laid on the larvae of horntail wasps or longhorn beetles. Adults are active in July and August, which is when one appeared all too briefly on dead wood up the garden in 2008. This is a widespread species found in coniferous or mixed woodland and is easily identified, unlike the vast majority of the family. The identification problem perhaps explains why what is a very handsome family has never been anything like so popular with entomologists as bees or aculeate wasps. None were included in the Red Data Book published in 1987 classifying endangered,

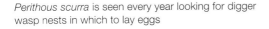

Perithous scurra is seen every year looking for digger wasp nests in which to lay eggs

Netelia species are nocturnal ichneumons and attracted to light. They used to come into the kitchen now and then but have not been seen for years. *Netelia* need treating with respect because they can bite

vulnerable and rare invertebrates in Britain but the assumption must be that a significant number of them are rare or endangered.

A hefty number of ichneumons, and all the Ichneumoninae sub-family, parasitise moth or butterfly species, laying their eggs in larvae or pupae; adult emergence is always from the pupa. None of these need the long ovipositors required by wood and stem-boring ichneumons. The decline in moth numbers over the last 20 years is a cause for concern for the parasites as well as the hosts, but has not been caused by the former. The social wasp mimics *Ichneumon xanthorius* and *Ichneumon sarcitorius* are seen fairly frequently, usually seeking nectar. *Ichneumon suspiciosus* has

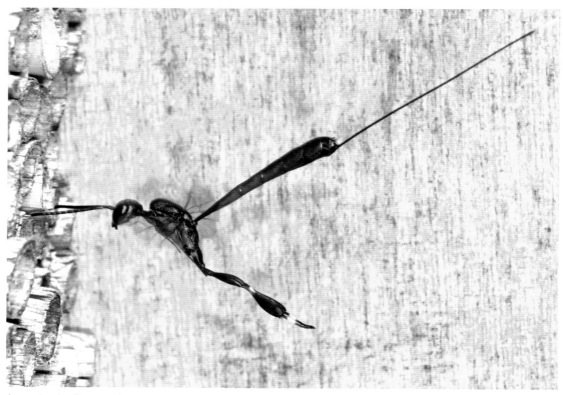

A spectacular *Gasteruption jaculator* female, one of two which spent hours checking out the Schwegler bee box in 2012 in the hope of finding nests of the bees *Heriades truncorum* or *Hylaeus communis* in which to lay eggs

markings dashing enough to set it apart from all its kin but has been observed only once in the garden.

One species which is host specific, and seemingly can have a massive impact on populations of the victim, is *Listrodromus nycthemerus*. They target Holly Blue butterfly caterpillars, laying an egg in first instar larvae. This results in the emergence of a single adult wasp from the normally formed Holly Blue pupa. Reportedly parasitism of larvae can reach 99 per cent, understandably causing a massive collapse in host populations. *Listrodromus nycthemerus* has been seen just once in the garden, even though the host is present every year. This is partly because the wasp takes up to seven years to reach peak numbers. One of the smaller ichneumons, measuring only two millimetres, is the stunning ant mimic *Gelis* species, spotted on

A *Gelis* species, a tiny ichneumon wasp that mimics ants

Some sawflies have bold colouring and one of the brightest is the Large Rose Sawfly *Arge pagana* with its orange abdomen

Wild Carrot attracts the Berberis Sawfly *Arge berberidis*

the ground in 2010. Chalcid wasps, from another superfamily of parasitoids that uses hosts from at least a dozen different insect families, often appear in the autumn.

Sawflies are not wasps but they are Hymenoptera and many are regarded as pests by horticulturalists and gardeners alike. There are more than 500 species in Britain, often striking in appearance but not always easy to identify. Unpopular ones because of the damage the larvae do to the leaves of fruit trees and bushes plus garden plants include the Apple Sawfly *Hoplocampa testudinea*, Turnip

SPECIES OF WASP RECORDED

CHRYSIDIDAE (CUCKOO WASPS)
Chrysis angustula
Chrysis ignita
Chrysis illigeri
Hedychridium roseum
Hedychrum niemelai
Pseudomalus auratus
Pseudomalus violaceus
Trichrysis cyanea

TIPHIIDAE (FLOWER WASPS)
Tiphia femorata

SAPYGIDAE (CLUB-HORNED WASPS)
Monosapyga clavicornis
Sapyga quinquepunctata

POMPILIDAE (SPIDER-HUNTING WASPS)
Agenioideus cinctellus
Anoplius infuscatus
Anoplius nigerrimus
Arachnospila anceps
Arachnospila spissa
Arachnospila trivialis
Auplopus carbonarius

Caliadurgus fasciatellus
Dipogon subintermedius
Dipogon variegatus
Priocnemis exaltata
Priocnemis parvula
Priocnemis perturbator

VESPIDAE (SOCIAL, POTTER AND MASON WASPS)
Common Wasp *Vespula vulgaris*
German Wasp *Vespula germanica*
Hornet *Vespa crabro*
Mason wasp *Ancistrocerus gazella*
Mason wasp *Ancistrocerus nigricornis*
Mason wasp *Ancistrocerus trifasciatus*
Mason wasp *Gymnomerus laevipes*
Mason wasp *Symmorphus bifasciatus*
Median Wasp *Dolichovespula media*
Saxon Wasp *Dolichovespula saxonica*
Tree Wasp *Dolichovespula sylvestris*

CRABRONIDAE (DIGGER WASPS)
Argogorytes mystaceus
Astata boops
Cerceris arenaria

Sawfly *Athalia rosae*, Gooseberry Sawfly *Nematus ribesii* and Large Rose Sawfly *Arge pagana*. Similarly, the Berberis Sawfly *Arge berberidis* is a newcomer to Britain first identified in 2002 that uses Berberis and Oregon-grape to feed its young. The species is now widespread and adults were seen on my Wild Carrot in 2011 and 2012. So far the nearby Oregon-grape seems to have escaped their attentions. The Large Rose Sawfly has been spotted a number of times, including again on Wild Carrot in 2012, when I also saw what proved to be *Arge ustulata*.

Chalcid wasp, showing dazzling metallic colouring

Cerceris rybyensis

Crabro peltarius

Crossocerus annulipes

Crossocerus cetratus

Crossocerus distinguendus

Crossocerus megacephalus

Crossocerus ovalis

Crossocerus podagricus

Crossocerus pusillus

Ectemnius cavifrons

Ectemnius cephalotes

Ectemnius continuus

Ectemnius dives

Ectemnius lituratus

Entomognathus brevis

Gorytes laticinctus

Lestiphorus bicinctus

Lindenius panzeri

Mellinus arvensis

Mimumesa dahlbomi

Nysson spinosus

Nysson trimaculatus

Oxybelus uniglumis

Passaloecus corniger

Passaloecus gracilis

Passaloecus singularis

Pemphredon inornata

Pemphredon lugubris

Pemphredon morio

Philanthus triangulum

Psenulus pallipes

Rhopalum clavipes

Rhopalum coarctatum

Spilomena beata

Stigmus pendulus

Stigmus solskyi

Trypoxylon attenuatum

Trypoxylon clavicerum

Trypoxylon medium

PARASITIC WASPS

Ephialtes manifestator

Gasteruption assectator

Gasteruption jaculator

Ichneumon sarcitorius

Ichneumon suspiciosus

Ichneumon xanthorius

Listrodromus nycthemerus

Perithous scurra

Sabre Wasp *Rhyssa persuasoria*

Chapter 8
Flies

Female *Callicera aurata*, with distinctive white tips to the antennae. She appeared at the top of the garden in August 2009. There were only five records of this species in Surrey between 1934 and 1996 and it is still decidedly difficult to find

Flies (Diptera) are not so numerous as Hymenoptera in the British list but they are still plentiful, with 102 families containing more than 6,500 species. There are more than 7,000 Hymenoptera, mostly Parasitica, including ichneumon wasps. The vast majority of flies are identifiable only by experts, and sometimes not easily by them, so for garden watchers the best focus of attention has always been a colourful, quite sizeable and numerically modest family of fewer than 300 species, the hoverflies (Syrphidae). The name by which they are colloquially known in the United States, flower flies, gives the game away and I have become a big fan over the last few years.

Surrey has more than 200 of the national list of hoverflies, and just over a quarter of them, 58 to be precise, have turned up in my garden. They are usually seen on flowers because although hoverflies are rightly praised as beneficial in predating pest species, this is done not by the adults, who rely generally on nectar and pollen for sustenance, but by their larvae. These utilise a wide range of feeding matter, including ground-layer and arboreal aphids, detritus or larvae in wasp and bee nests, roots, stems, bulbs and rhizomes, and sap runs on trees. The presence of ancient woodland close to the garden has undoubtedly helped boost the numbers since that is a habitat in which they thrive, particularly where there is decaying timber. Keeping a closer eye on flowers from March to October in 2012 also helped boost the tally, with around a dozen new species noted. Seeing good numbers of these lively flies on a sunny summer's day is always a pleasure and the tendency a few have to hover straight in front of one's face, as if checking out an interloper, is appealing.

Some of the visitors have been nationally scarce. Male and female *Callicera aurata*, a Red

Brachypalpoides lentus is one of the larger hoverflies and the pictured male is the only one I have seen. Almost certainly he strayed in from the park

Data Book species with distinctive white tips to the antennae, have both been seen in the last few years, with the female on dead wood and the male on a plant for which, perhaps surprisingly, it seems to have an affinity – Firethorn. The larvae live in rot holes in Beech or Birch, both of which trees are common in the adjacent park. The scarce bumblebee mimic *Criorhina ranunculi* is a spring species that has the same requirement for rotting wood in Beech and Birch; they visit various flowers including Cherry Laurel and it was on this plant that I saw one in the garden in 2007. The impressive and far from common red and black species *Brachypalpoides lentus*, which appeared in 2009, is associated with decaying Beech and Oak. In contrast, *Scaeva selenitica*, a partial migrant seen once also in 2009, has a connection with coniferous woodland. Possibly this one was just passing through, though there is a smallish plantation of conifers in the park only 100 metres from the garden. (The commonest member of the genus found in Britain, *Scaeva pyrastri*, is also migratory and is seen in the garden virtually every year though not in 2012.)

Male *Cheilosia caerulescens* on Bidens in July 2012. This species is a recent arrival in the United Kingdom

Didea fasciata is a formerly scarce species which I had not seen until this male arrived to take nectar from Ivy in the front garden in October 2012

To be fully effective, bumblebee mimicry needs to involve an invertebrate's being fairly large and carrying plenty of hair. The species shown on this spread fit both bills but not all of them are regular visitors. They are *Volucella bombylans plumata* female (1), *Eristalis intricarius* male (2), *Cheilosia illustrata* female (3) and the Greater Bulb Fly *Merodon equestris* (pale form female 4, mating pair 5)

Two more bumblebee mimics, neither commonplace – a *Criorhina ranunculi* female on Cherry Laurel and a fresh *Criorhina floccosa* male on Bramley's Seedling apple blossom

Arguably the most imposing genus of hoverflies is *Volucella*, whose members are mostly large wasp or bee mimics that always provide a thrill when they arrive. All five species on the British list, three of which are nationally scarce, have visited the garden, with such flowers as Wild Carrot, Cotoneaster and Canadian Goldenrod proving popular for gathering nectar. Four of the five have a close link with the nests of social bees and wasps; the exception is *Volucella inflata*, which seemingly uses sap runs on trees attacked by the Goat Moth *Cossus cossus*. The largest *Volucella*, which makes a tremendous buzzing sound in flight, is *Volucella zonaria*, a Hornet mimic that has extended its range considerably in the last 60 years. There were a lot of these around in the summer of 2012, possibly through migration from mainland Europe – they can be pretty mobile, facing no problems flying long distances due to their size and strength. Larvae have been found in the nests of the Common Wasp and German Wasp, a comment which also applies to *Volucella inanis* and *Volucella pellucens*. The last-named, the commonest of the genus, is not a wasp mimic in colouring and not greatly like a bee either since it is not hairy and the markings are slightly 'off'. A more exact bee mimic and also quite readily seen is *Volucella bombylans*. This one is hairy, has two colour forms and uses not only social wasp nests but also those of bumblebees, in which the larvae apparently scavenge debris and sometimes attack the resident grubs.

Similarly excellent bumblebee mimics include *Criorhina floccosa* (a commoner species than *Criorhina ranunculi*), *Eristalis intricarius* – one of five members of that genus to have visited the garden – and *Merodon equestris*. The last-named, though handsome, is by no means the gardener's friend as the colloquial name Greater Bulb Fly confirms. They are believed to have arrived in Britain at the end of the 19th

Scaeva pyrastri, with its almost ghostly markings, and the yellower *Scaeva selenitica* are both partially migratory but while the former is seen virtually every year *Scaeva selenitica* is nationally scarce and has turned up only once

The best social wasp mimics among hoverflies are three imposing members of the *Volucella* genus shown here. For the record, despite the similarity in looks, no hoverflies have a sting, nor do they bite. *Volucella zonaria* (bottom) looks like a Hornet in size as well as colouring and uses various social wasp nests for breeding. So does *Volucella inanis* (below), whose face is as strikingly marked as all the members of the genus. Both are pictured on Canadian Goldenrod. The last of the trio, *Volucella inflata* (right), seemingly uses sap runs for its progeny

Most wasp mimics among hoverflies are in the Syrphini tribe, which generally is brightly coloured. The *Chrysotoxum cautum* male (left) is an extreme example, whereas the *Chrysotoxum festivum* female (above) and *Chrysotoxum bicinctum* female (below) have less pronounced markings. Larvae are believed to have an association with ant nests

Three more wasp mimics from the Syrphini tribe. *Syrphus vitripennis* (right, a female) is common, along with the similarly marked *Syrphus ribesii*. *Dasysyrphus albostriatus* (below, male) is also seen quite often but *Dasysyrphus tricinctus* (below right, female) has appeared only a handful of times

century in bulbs brought over from Holland. One of their prime targets, but not the only one, is Daffodil bulbs, which their larvae eat and reside in for ten months before pupating in the soil. Adults have several bumblebee mimic colour forms but all are very hairy and are usually seen in late spring, tending to last less than three weeks. After being far from obvious for several years they were present in good numbers in June 2012, visiting flowers particularly from the *Asteraceae* family. One pair afforded excellent views of mating, during which event the male beat his wings with remarkable rapidity.

There are numerous other perceived wasp mimics which, unlike the *Volucella* brigade, do not impact on the nests of the species they resemble. Their colouring, which in a number of cases is orange and black rather than yellow and black, presumably benefits them by putting off predators though a number of digger wasps catch these mimics to stock their nests. Among the species to have been in the garden, all of them attractive and all a reasonable size, are *Helophilus pendulus*, *Chrysotoxum bicinctum*, *Chrysotoxum cautum*, *Chrysotoxum festivum*, *Dasysyrphus tricinctus*, *Dasysyrphus venustus*, the Marmalade Hoverfly *Episyrphus balteatus* (probably the commonest of them all), *Eupeodes corollae*, *Eupeodes luniger*,

Meliscaeva auricollis, Meliscaeva cinctella, Myathropa florea, Sphaerophoria scripta, Syrphus ribesii, Syrphus vitripennis and *Xanthogramma pedissequum.*

The majority of this list are seen every year and sometimes exclusively on flowers in the borders, which have also attracted eight members of the more monochrome *Cheilosia* genus, the largest in Britain with more than 30 species. The exception was a female *Cheilosia*

A mating pair of *Sphaerophoria scripta* (left), one of the commonest hoverflies in the garden. Males are distinctive because the abdomen is much longer than the wings

Meliscaeva cinctella (below) is one of the smaller Syrphini. This is a male on Wild Carrot, showing a trait of the genus in having his wings open

Two members of the *Epistrophe* genus – a male *Epistrophe eligans* (above) on flowering Cherry and a female *Epistrophe grossulariae* (left) on Canadian Goldenrod. Both species are seen each year in the garden but never in great numbers

illustrata, a bumblebee mimic seen on a leaf at the top of the garden in July 2012. *Cheilosia illustrata* uses the umbellifer Common Hogweed, which was in the garden for a few years in the 1990s, for breeding and *Cheilosia* species seem to have an affinity for another member of that family, Wild Carrot. The rarest visitor from this genus was a male *Cheilosia caerulescens*, which was seen taking nectar from Bidens flowers on a single day in July 2012. This is a new species to Britain, first confirmed here in 2006 after expanding its range dramatically in Europe since 1980. They are viewed as a pest by gardeners because, like *Merodon equestris* but unlike the majority of hoverflies, their larvae feed on and can ruin a popular garden plant, in this instance *Sempervivum* or House Leek.

Six other species are worth mentioning, three of which were newcomers in 2012. *Rhingia* species are unmistakable because they have a definite 'snout'. *Rhingia campestris*, seen only a couple of times since 2005, is common nationally and the larvae are associated with

Eupeodes luniger can be seen for most of the year. This female is taking nectar from Oregon-grape

Female *Xanthogramma pedissequum* (right), a personal favourite because the black and yellow markings tend to be more intense than with many hoverflies, resembling those of potter and mason wasps. No precise mimicry of this wasp family has been proved, and the hoverflies have been bred from ant nests

Syritta pipiens (above) is small, common and distinctive because of the noticeably swollen hind femora in both sexes – this is a female

Eristalis species often look much redder in flight than when settled but this male Drone Fly *Eristalis tenax* (right) had bright markings whatever the action or location

With a cream band on the abdomen and dark wing patches, *Leucozona lucorum* (below) is a striking but irregular species in the garden. This is a female

cow dung, whereas those of the scarcer and more brightly coloured *Rhingia rostrata* may be connected with Badger latrines. Until a female appeared on Fleabane in the border at the end of August 2012, pictured at the start of this chapter, I had never seen one of these lovely little flies, which seem to be increasing in number nationally but are still uncommon in Surrey. Another female, or maybe the same one, turned up on Ivy in the autumn. Two 'hits' in one year was worth celebrating.

Sericomyia silentis, a large hoverfly which is

only local in incidence in Surrey and had not been recorded from this part of the county before, appeared in September 2012 taking nectar from Ivy flowers in the front garden. Then at the start of October, confirming how worthwhile it can be just to spend time watching what arrives on flowers, a male *Didea fasciata*, formerly scarce nationally and another local species in the county, turned up on the Ivy. That one's larvae are believed to feed on aphids on Scots Pine *Pinus sylvestris*, of which there are several examples nearby.

Xylota species are linked to rotting vegetation, principally timber. However, nearly all the plentiful *Xylota segnis* found in the garden have been on or near the compost bins (they visit flowers only rarely), suggesting that the contents perhaps provide a good habitat. If this is the case, the steady increase in composting by households may stand the species in good stead. The same applies to *Syritta pipiens*, a common but pretty little species with a distinctively enlarged hind femur and one definitely linked to compost.

Rhingia campestris is darker than *Rhingia rostrata* and with a slightly longer snout. They have been seen in the garden several times, including when this female basked on my side of the fence on a neighbour's Buddleja

They are seen for much of the year, certainly from June to October, and do take nectar.

The numerous other flies seen in the garden cannot be detailed in full because many have not been identified. There are some fascinating species though, starting with predatory robberflies, which feed off a wide range of invertebrates. These flies are fairly frequent on

Badger latrines are a possible breeding location for *Rhingia rostrata* but to emphasise how ignorant we still are about so many invertebrates, there was no knowing where this female full of eggs in mid-October 2012 was going to lay them

A *Chrysogaster solstitialis* (above), showing the huge red eyes that are a hallmark of the species

A *Xylota segnis* (left) taking a break in the sun on dead wood near the compost bin, a customary site. This species is commoner in the garden than the other pictured hoverfly, *Xylota sylvarum* (below left), which has yellow rather than red on the abdomen

open acid grassland in the adjacent park but less so in the garden. The two which I have spotted are the Stripe-legged Robberfly virtually every year and the Kite-tailed Robberfly a couple of times. Both species have had prey in their jaws and, given the number of potential victims found in flower borders, it is perhaps slightly surprising that more robberflies do not visit. The Stripe-legged Robberfly preys not just on Diptera but also on small- to medium-sized Hymenoptera so gardens are perfect for them. Dance flies look very like robberflies. They hunt far and wide and the largest and commonest, *Empis tessellata*, can be seen most years in the garden, especially on Wild Carrot. As often as not, mating occurs after the male has gifted a prey item to the female.

Robberflies are terribly effective predators. Here the only two species seen in the garden are on display with prey, the Kite-tailed Robberfly (left) and a gravid Stripe-legged Robberfly (below)

Dark-edged Bee-flies (above) are entirely a spring species and can be seen flying fast and then hovering close to the ground to spray around some of their massive stock of eggs in the hope that the resulting progeny will be able to find a nesting bee, wasp or beetle

Dance flies *Empis tessellata* mating (left), with the female eating a gift presented to her by the male

Robberflies (Asilidae) and dance flies (Empididae) are from the Brachycera suborder of Diptera, which also includes bee-flies (Bombylidae), snipeflies (Rhagionidae), soldierflies (Stratiomyidae), horseflies (Tabanidae), stiletto-flies (Therevidae), bluebottles (Calliphoridae) and long-legged flies (Dolichopodidae). The Dark-edged Bee-fly is seen every spring either taking nectar with its remarkably long proboscis or hovering above the ground. The latter action is connected with egg-laying since bee-fly larvae eat solitary bee and wasp larvae as well as some beetle larvae. The method is distinctly speculative since female bee-flies lay large numbers of tiny eggs on the ground in the hope that some of the resulting larvae will find a host nest nearby to enter or an adult in transit to latch on to for the same purpose. The

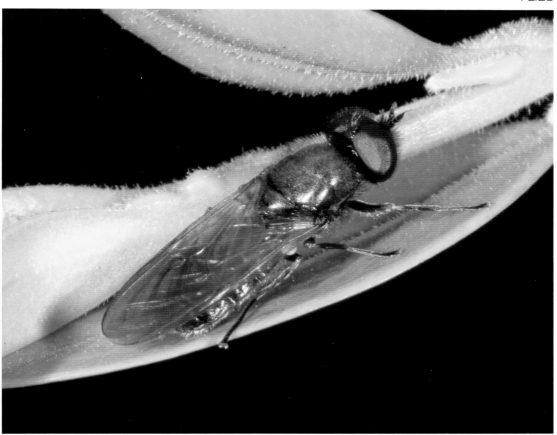

Soldierflies can be tremendously colourful and here are two fine examples. The male Broad Centurion (above) mixes green and bronze while the female Twin-spot Centurion (left) has a dazzling combination of red, blue, bronze and black

vast majority of the eggs and larvae fail but as its name suggests, this stoutly-built fly is common, sometimes abundant, and can be seen in virtually any habitat, including gardens. Clearly the laying tactic works even though it is by definition hit and miss.

As the name suggests, stiletto-flies are reasonably long and skinny. They are also hairy and, despite some comments to the contrary, are not proven to be predatory. One of the commoner species, *Thereva nobilitata*, has lovely golden hair and can be seen most years in the garden albeit only in passing, usually sunbathing on a leaf in July or August. Less agreeable to humans because they pack a nasty bite is *Haematopota pluvialis*, a cleg fly from the horsefly tribe, with remarkable and diagnostic

Bites by the cleg fly *Haematopota pluvialis* are painful but one can almost forgive the transgression when studying the insect's remarkable eyes

A fresh female stiletto-fly *Thereva nobilitata* sunbathing

Not a popular fly though it is attractive – the bluebottle *Calliphora vicina*

multi-coloured eyes. They appear most years. The horsefly *Tabanus bromus* is only an occasional visitor and overall this family is not well represented locally, which may be as well for the comfort of people spending time outside.

Soldierflies too are not easily found in the vicinity of the garden, which is a shame because they are attractive, with a good range of colours. Many species are suited by damper habitats than obtain around Reigate but several have appeared, including the dead ones brought back to her nest by the solitary wasp *Crossocerus megacephalus* mentioned in the previous chapter. Live species in 2012 were a male Broad Centurion and a female Twin-spot Centurion, a species with marvellous markings. The colloquial names of soldierflies are always rather jolly, with a military connection – examples are the Ornate Brigadier Soldierfly and the Banded General Soldierfly.

The Dark-edged Bee-fly is one parasite of insects and there are plenty more. Those that deal with bees and/or wasps are led by one that I had not recorded in the garden until 2012 – the so-called thick-headed fly *Myopa pellucida*, a nationally rare member of a genus that is widespread but not commonly seen. They are Conopid flies and parasitoids or internal parasites of adult mining bees, with females skulking on flowers or vegetation until a potential host appears. They then move

Myopa pellucida (left) is a nationally scarce parasitic thick-headed fly that seeks out solitary mining bee adults in which to lay her eggs. *Sicus ferrugineus* (below), similarly marked though with a completely pale face, is altogether commoner. This species has a habit of pairing, as here, without necessarily mating, perhaps because the male is protecting his sperm post-coitus

swiftly to intercept the bee, sometimes in flight, and open the abdomen to insert an egg. The resulting larva eats the host from within, pupating in the void that is left once growing has finished.

My first sighting of a *Myopa pellucida* was in early April when one patrolled a Cherry Laurel hedge and went for just about everything that settled including, intriguingly, some hoverflies. The second specimen – or perhaps the same one – was on a Box bush near which several *Andrena* mining bees were nesting in mid-May. Other flies from this family that use the same

This *Leopoldius signatus* female (left) gave tremendous value in October 2012 though the social wasps she was trying to find to lay her eggs in were lacking in numbers and size after a poor summer

Three more thick-headed flies. *Conops quadrifasciatus* (left) is quite a regular visitor but both *Conops ceriaeformis* (female, below left) and *Physocephala rufipes* (male, below), with its extreme wasp-like waist, have been noted only once each. *Conops* species use wasps and/or bees but *Physocephala rufipes* seemingly goes just for bees

method of search and attack and have been seen waiting for bees, including bumblebees, or wasps are *Sicus ferrugineus* and the excellent wasp mimics *Conops quadrifasciatus*, *Conops ceriaeformis*, *Leopoldius signatus* and *Physocephala rufipes*. *Sicus ferrugineus* is guaranteed each year. As a group, the others are less frequently seen though my Ivy hosted a male and female *Leopoldius signatus* for a fortnight in October 2012. That was the first record of the species for the garden and for this part of Surrey.

Since there are only 24 species of Conopidae nationally, it is pleasing to have had six in the garden at one point or another, especially as they are not always easy to spot despite the often bright colouration. They have really caught my imagination with their handsome appearance and fascinating life cycles, not least because although looking relatively flimsy their ability to hijack aculeates that are larger and much better armed proves they are as tough as old boots.

Parasites or parasitoids that attack other

Tachinid flies, many of which show beautiful colouring, are parasitic on a wide range of invertebrate species. Those shown here, all of them quite sizeable, are *Tachina fera* (1) on Wild Carrot, *Nowickia ferox* (2) on Fleabane, *Eriothrix rufomaculata* (3) on Common Ragwort – a popular plant for tachinids – and *Dexiosoma caninum* (4). The first three are not in short supply but *Dexiosoma caninum* is locally uncommon

Female *Eustalomyia hilaris*, a cuckoo fly looking for egg-laying opportunities in a solitary wasp's nest

families of invertebrate include the tachinid flies *Eriothrix rufomaculatus*, *Dexiosoma caninum*, *Gymnosoma rotundatum*, *Nowickia ferox* and *Tachina fera*, all of which are striking physically. Larvae of *Eriothrix rufomaculatus*, *Nowickia ferox* and *Tachina fera* feed on moth caterpillars. *Dexiosoma caninum*, nationally widespread but seen only a handful of times in Surrey, is believed to use chafer beetle larvae and *Gymnosoma rotundatum* definitely goes for shieldbugs.

Gymnosoma rotundatum, a really attractive fly, is not too hard to find in Surrey and Sussex but is decidedly uncommon in most of England and is classified as a Red Data Book species. Males and females are regular visitors to flowers, notably Wild Carrot. Breeding sees an egg laid on a nymph or adult shieldbug, normally the Green Shieldbug or Gorse Shieldbug, and this spends the winter developing inside the host in larval form before pupating in the ground. Digger wasps have their fly parasites too – a couple of examples are the grey and black Anthomyiid flies *Eustalomyia festiva*, which I have seen several times, and *Eustalomyia hilaris*, which is

altogether scarcer and provided only the fifth sighting in Surrey when going up and down a standing log looking for host nests in July 2012. Both flies are cuckoos of *Ectemnius cavifrons* among other species.

As the name suggests, the Yellow Dung Fly can usually be seen on faeces, in which its larvae live. The adults are hunters though,

Yellow Dung Flies are very hairy, and adept predators

preying on small flies. In turn they are one of the prey species of the digger wasp *Mellinus arvensis*. The Noon Fly *Mesembrina meridiana* presumably takes its English name from the second part of the Latin name but since they can be seen at almost any time of day the title is questionable. It is a common species often seen taking nectar at flowers from spring right through to autumn and lays eggs mostly in cow dung. The larvae are carnivorous.

Maintaining the scatological connection, tiny ensign flies, which usually have their wings spread open, also use dung – the Latin name for the genus, *Sepsis*, rather tells the story – and are very common in the garden. St Mark's Flies are usually noticeable around the saint's day near the end of April when males can swarm in thousands, their characteristic long legs hanging down below them. The larvae of this fly feed on vegetation in the soil but the adults are often seen in gardens and are noted as useful pollinators of some fruit trees.

Britain has more than 300 species of crane-fly and arguably the one most noticed around human habitation is *Tipula paludosa*,

A Noon Fly on Ivy, showing the striking colouring

which as a winged adult emerges from the ground – often lawns or verges – in early autumn. They frequently come into homes at night, not entirely to the delight of residents. Females carry more than 200 eggs and the resultant larvae are the notorious leatherjackets. These, usually measuring 20 to 30 millimetres, are beloved of Rooks and Crows as tasty and often plentiful morsels but unpopular with gardeners. They eat the roots and even stems of grasses, leading potentially to brown patches on a lawn.

An ensign fly with numerous unwanted passengers in the form of mites hitching a lift. It is debatable whether he or she would have been capable of flying far carrying this load

SPECIES OF HOVERFLY RECORDED

Brachypalpoides lentus	Eupeodes corollae
Callicera aurata	Eupeodes luniger
Cheilosia caerulescens	Ferdinandea cuprea
Cheilosia illustrata	Helophilus pendulus
Cheilosia impressa	Leucozona lucorum
Cheilosia pagana	Melanostoma scalare
Cheilosia proxima	Meliscaeva auricollis
Cheilosia scutellata	Meliscaeva cinctella
Cheilosia soror	Merodon equestris
Cheilosia vernalis	Myathropa florea
Cheilosia vulpina	Platycheirus albimanus
Chrysogaster solstitialis	Platycheirus scutatus
Chrysotoxum bicinctum	Rhingia campestris
Chrysotoxum cautum	Rhingia rostrata
Chrysotoxum festivum	Scaeva pyrastri
Criorhina floccosa	Scaeva selenitica
Criorhina ranunculi	Sericomyia silentis
Dasysyrphus albostriatus	Sphaerophoria scripta
Dasysyrphus tricinctus	Syritta pipiens
Dasysyrphus venustus	Syrphus ribesii
Didea fasciata	Syrphus vitripennis
Epistrophe eligans	Volucella bombylans
Epistrophe grossulariae	Volucella inanis
Episyrphus balteatus	Volucella inflata
Eristalis arbustorum	Volucella pellucens
Eristalis interruptus	Volucella zonaria
Eristalis intricarius	Xanthogramma pedissequum
Eristalis pertinax	Xylota segnis
Eristalis tenax	Xylota sylvarum

OTHER SPECIES OF FLY RECORDED

Anthomyiid fly *Eustalomyia festiva*
Anthomyiid fly *Eustalomyia hilaris*
Bluebottle *Calliphora vicina*
Broad Centurion *Chloromyia formosa*
Cleg fly *Haematopota pluvialis*
Conopid fly *Conops quadrifasciatus*
Conopid fly *Conops ceriaeformis*
Conopid fly *Leopoldius signatus*
Conopid fly *Myopa pellucida*
Conopid fly *Physocephala rufipes*
Conopid fly *Sicus ferrugineus*
Crane-fly *Tipula paludosa*
Dance fly *Empis tessellata*
Dark-edged Bee-fly *Bombylius major*
Ensign fly *Sepsis* sp
Horsefly *Tabanus bromius*
Kite-tailed Robberfly *Machimus atricapillus*
Noon Fly *Mesembrina meridiana*
Semaphore Fly *Poecilobothrus nobilitatus*
Stiletto-fly *Thereva nobilitata*
St Mark's Fly *Bibio marci*
Stripe-legged Robberfly *Dioctria baumhaueri*
Tachinid fly *Dexiosoma caninum*
Tachinid fly *Eriothrix rufomaculatus*
Tachinid fly *Gymnosoma rotundatum*
Tachinid fly *Nowickia ferox*
Tachinid fly *Tachina fera*
Twin-spot Centurion *Sargus bipunctatus*
Yellow Dung Fly *Scathophaga stercoraria*
Yellow-legged Black *Pachygaster leachii*

A crane-fly *Tipula paludosa* (left) emerging one autumn in the 1990s from the front lawn where the larva, known as a leatherjacket, had eaten its fill of grass roots and stems

St Mark's Flies (right) can be useful pollinators of fruit trees and, in keeping with that profile, this pair is mating on Apple blossom

Chapter 9
Beetles

There are nothing like so many individual beetles on the planet as there are ants, but they are by far the most numerous insect family in terms of species, with around 370,000 worldwide (plus many yet to be discovered) and roughly 4,000 in Britain. With damage to a number of our wild habitats continuing, they are under pressure nationally, with 250 of the total not having been seen since the 1970s, but it is worth pointing out that the vast majority do not make their presence obvious. There are exceptions, chiefly the ladybird family (Coccinellidae), which, apart from in the notorious swarms of 1976, tends to receive a good press. To an extent this is

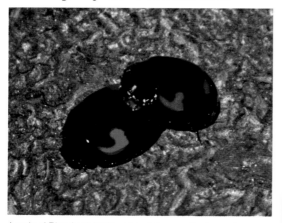

A pair of Pine Ladybirds, one of the smallest species

The Cream-spot Ladybird is medium-sized

because the larvae of most species eat aphids, never a popular insect with gardeners. Solitary wasps also sort out large numbers of aphids but what sets ladybirds apart is that they are mobile predators as both larvae and adults.

The commonest of the nine species seen in the garden over the years is the Seven-spot Ladybird, females of which lay up to 200 eggs beneath leaves close to colonies of aphids. The resulting larvae, which are a fair bit longer than the adults at around 11 millimetres, forage ferociously for three weeks or so before pupating. They have done very good work on runner beans in the garden for years. Seven-spot Ladybirds, like all the others, are effective if slightly ungainly fliers and they last a long time, overwintering, often in large numbers, under tree bark or in any other insulated and secure spot.

Ladybirds have few predators since the bold colouring they carry denotes danger, in this instance the fact that they taste unpleasant thanks to alkaloid poisons. Colour variation in individual species can be considerable and cause confusion to observers, who think they have more species in a garden than they actually do. As an example, the usual form of the Two-spot Ladybird is mostly red with black spots but some are mostly black with red spots. Others are orange or yellow, and there can be more than two spots. In contrast, the Fourteen-spot Ladybird does not show much variation, with yellow and black consistently shown.

Not all the 40-plus species in Britain eat invertebrates – the Twenty-two-spot Ladybird relies on fungus or mildew and this one is not necessarily so helpful to gardeners since the beetles can pick up parts of what they are feeding on, including spores, and unwittingly transfer them to other plants. The Twenty-two-spot is very common. Some ladybirds are generalists in the flora they use for living and breeding on, others are a tad more specific, such as the Pine Ladybird and Cream-streaked Ladybird. These are aphid eaters, though Pine Ladybird larvae also consume scale insects, and they concentrate on evergreens. Despite

The Seven-spot Ladybird is probably the commonest native species. Left, a larva with plenty of aphid prey to eat. Above, the adult emerging – they are always coloured yellow at this stage. Below, an adult with the distinctive red and black hue

The Cream-streaked Ladybird, first found in Britain in 1939, is local in incidence in Surrey and breeds on pine trees

the specific name, Pine Ladybirds turned up in reasonable numbers in the garden in 2007 on Cherry Laurel. The Cream-streaked Ladybird is seen much less often.

The villain of the story is the non-native Harlequin Ladybird, which is Asian in origin and was introduced to Europe as a medium of pest control but, as so often when humans interfere with nature, the supposed controller has become more of a pest itself. This species, which has more than 20 colour forms, most of which involve a fair bit of pale marking up front, is spreading rapidly across the countryside and poses a major threat to some of our native species. The trouble is that it outpoints ours in both size and productivity – Harlequin Ladybirds seem capable of producing three broods in one year granted favourable conditions. Moreover, they not only use the same prey species as our natives but can also utilise other ladybirds, butterfly larvae, hoverfly larvae and lacewings.

According to a study across Europe by the Centre for Ecology and Hydrology published in 2012, the impact has already been dismal, with a 44 per cent decline in the Two-spot Ladybird in Britain. Predictably, given the scale of the problem, Harlequin Ladybirds have made their presence felt at my house, especially when virtually swarming a couple of times in the autumn, with more than 100 visible on the front of the building. It is hard to see what, if anything, can be done to halt the unwanted progress of this species.

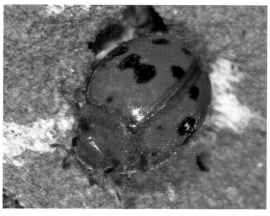

The Twenty-four-spot Ladybird is a vegetarian species

Two small ladybird species that are predominantly yellow: a mating pair of Twenty-two-spots (above) and a Fourteen-spot (right)

   With the majority of beetles I tend to be lazier than ideal, focussing principally on those which are large, colourful or both, but as plenty of beetles meet those criteria there is no shortage of suitable subject matter. Nine species seen in the garden, all but one since 2004, were formerly, or still are, nationally scarce, reflecting the proximity of the property to the ancient woodland in the park – many beetles are saproxylic, using decayed wood, or rely on living trees. Longhorn beetles are a particular favourite and two with bright markings are seen most years. The Black and Yellow Longhorn is a great basker on foliage or flowers and flies in a noticeably undulating manner. In common with many others, their larvae feed on decaying deciduous wood, a comment which equally applies to Wasp Beetles, shown mating at the start of this chapter. Their mimicry of social wasps must be useful; larvae are often found in Willow or Birch. The Two-banded Longhorn is fairly common nationwide but the chunky Tanner Beetle, which was noticed on a log in 2009, seems to be declining. A pair that used to be designated as scarce are the Spruce Shortwing Longhorn, with its distinctive swollen femora, which has been seen a couple of times, and the more regular Speckled Longhorn.

   Tanner Beetle larvae feed on the roots of the host trees, mostly Beech, Birch and Oak, or on stumps, while those of the Spruce Shortwing Longhorn and Two-banded Longhorn are associated with conifers. The Speckled Longhorn is less specific, using either deciduous or coniferous wood. One of the

The villain of the piece, though through no fault of its own: the Harlequin Ladybird in a red form (above, left) and a dark form (above). Left, one of the principal victims of this alien's arrival, a mating pair of Two-spot Ladybirds

smaller and widespread members of the longhorn tribe, with an intriguing two-year life cycle, is the Fairy-ring Longhorn Beetle. One appeared on a rose flower in 2012. Their larvae seemingly feed for up to two years on mycelium in humus infested by *Marasmius oreades*, or the Fairy-ring Fungus. Eight months earlier, an almost perfect Fairy Ring – the first I had ever noticed in the garden – had appeared around the Magnolia tree 15 metres from where the beetle turned up. How closely connected the two events were, if indeed they were connected at all, is a matter for conjecture. The beetle is relatively common.

Moving away from longhorns, one stunning species that appeared all too briefly on a piece of dead wood while I was watching solitary wasps in the summer of 2011 was the Oak Jewel Beetle, also known as the Two-spot Wood-borer. This one used to be rare, given a status of RDB 2 (vulnerable) in the 1987 Red Data Book for insects, but has been increasing in numbers ever since the infamous storm of October that year. It is associated with mature Oak trees and by inference with the worrying

disease known as Sudden Oak Death but there is no proof that the beetle causes the disease. Oak Jewel Beetles probably accelerate the damaging effects by infesting trees already 'under the influence' since the larvae feed on the inner bark. Another striking species that is still scarce is the Black-headed Cardinal Beetle, which was seen a couple of times near the end of the garden in the early 1990s. The Red-headed version is commoner nationally and that one has been spotted more recently, in 2005 and 2008.

One of the rarer beetles seen on wood in the garden is the unobtrusive little bark beetle *Platypus cylindricus*, formerly a Red Data Book species but subsequently demoted to nationally scarce. Also scarce, ten times the size, and the most iconic beetle in Britain, is the Stag Beetle, which breeds in the nearby park. This spectacular insect, highlighted by the male's astonishing 'antlers', which are actually mandibles, holds a strong position in British folklore. Stories about their being responsible for thunder and lightning, or flying about with hot coals in their jaws to set buildings alight,

Longhorns are among the most attractive beetles, and the Black and Yellow (left), pictured on a runner bean leaf, is one of the more brightly coloured. The Tanner Beetle (above) is the largest longhorn to have turned up; they use deciduous trees whereas the Two-banded Longhorn (below) is at home on conifers

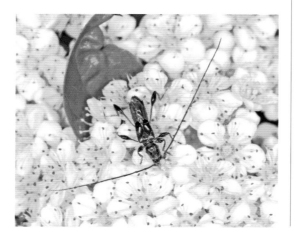

Firethorn blossom is attractive for the Speckled Longhorn Beetle (above) and Spruce Shortwing Longhorn Beetle (below). The enlarged femora on the legs of the latter species are clearly visible

are risible to us but show just how nature could affect the minds of superstitious people in bygone days. Being part of folklore does nothing to guarantee survival in the modern era however, and sadly the Stag Beetle has suffered a serious decline in population in Britain over the last 40 years or so. This is due mainly to habitat loss or fragmentation and a shortage of old-style woodland management. The Stag Beetle has protected status, listed on Schedule 5 of the Wildlife and Countryside Act 1981 and Annex II of the EC Habitats Directive, and is a UK Biodiversity Action Plan species.

Females, which lack the antlers though they do still have pronounced mandibles, had been spotted in the garden a few times in June or July, the months when the species is most active, but until 2012 no males had visited, or at least been seen. This was slightly surprising since they are often found in pursuit of females. Whatever the reason, my luck changed at the end of June when a lovely male measuring 60 millimetres turned up, enabling me to study him closely before release to a safe, concealed place in daylight – they are essentially nocturnal. The exercise confirmed what impressive and supremely handsome creatures Stag Beetles are. A memorable experience for me, though quite what he thought of it is open to debate. Stag Beetles have a long life cycle, four to six years

Lesser Stag Beetles (left) – this is a female – are significantly smaller, and much commoner, than Stag Beetles

The Fairy-ring Fungus that appeared around the Magnolia in 2011 was followed the year after by the appearance of a Fairy-ring Longhorn Beetle, a species that spends its larval stages eating the fungus

according to the Natural History Museum, and this time is spent mostly as larvae. These can measure up to 11 centimetres in exceptional cases and always reside in decayed wood, particularly Oak. Hence the need for good woodland management.

Stag Beetles are effective fliers but do not always land so well. The same applies to another large beetle, the 30-millimetre Cockchafer or May-bug. This is related to dung beetles and like many chafers is often regarded as a pest since the grubs eat roots in the soil for at least three years and the adults eat leaves on deciduous trees. The numbers seen in Britain, though, can hardly make the Cockchafer an economic threat. Adults are seen, as the name suggests, mainly in May and they fly rather noisily and clumsily at night, making them a tad daunting to householders if coming through an open window as has happened a few times at home.

Another chafer to appear most years is the Summer Chafer, seen from June to August,

In June 2012 this superb male Stag Beetle (above), with characteristic colouring, ended a long wait for one to be found in the garden. Females (left) had been seen several times. The mouth parts or 'antlers' (below left) are a marvel of design and quality construction and it is to be hoped this chap was able to use them against other males in the days following his appearance

Female Rhinoceros Beetle, lacking the projection on the head which males have

A Cockchafer or May-bug on a fence early one morning

which has a shorter life cycle than the Cockchafer but still not a short one compared with many beetles. When trying to find mates they fly around tree tops at dusk or in the night, often in large numbers, and on occasions several have been found dead or dying in the pond the following morning, having fallen in exhausted. I have also seen a third chafer, the Garden Chafer, on plants in the pond but mostly on flower heads. They can be numerous and provide opportunities for a number of predators.

A second species in which, like the Stag Beetle, the male is more imposing than the female is the Rhinoceros Beetle. Frustratingly the only sightings in the garden have been females. Males of the Lesser Stag Beetle have small antlers and this species is commoner than its larger relative, appearing most years. Ground Beetles, including Violet Ground Beetles with their lovely colouring, are active at night and predatory, feeding on slugs and smaller invertebrates as well as fruit. They are able to defend themselves to some extent against predators by discharging acid from the abdomen and their armoury also includes the capacity to run fast when required. They are not seen regularly, mainly because my observations tend to be restricted to daylight hours. Lifting logs to see what is beneath may be effective as a means of discovering invertebrates but it never seems likely to be helpful to them.

Red-headed Cardinal Beetles are commoner than the Black-headed variety but are still not terribly frequent in the garden

Summer Chafer (left) and Garden Chafer (below), both of which turned up on Iris leaves in the pond

The brightness of some of their coats gives soldier beetles their name and *Cantharis rustica* is among the most frequently encountered in the garden. Adults, often found on umbellifers, and larvae are both predatory on small invertebrates. Plenty of garden visitors have equally bright colouring, including the Common Malachite, although most of the red is hidden at rest. They like flower heads, especially Wild Carrot. The Swollen-thighed Beetle is a pollen eater also likeliest to turn up on flower heads through spring and summer. They are common but always welcome because of the bright green colouring, though females show more blue.

Green and red smartly combine in the little leaf beetle *Gastrophysa polygoni*, which I have seen only once in the garden and on dead wood, not a plant. From the same family is the Rosemary Beetle, a southern European species which has migrated to Britain and is noted as a pest, eating such plants as Lavender,

Male Swollen-thighed Beetles (above) are readily seen on flower heads through the summer. Females (right) turn up much less often and have no enlargement of the legs

Rosemary, Sage and Thyme. Native, but equally unpopular in houses where its 'woolly bear' larvae eat fibres including carpets, is the Varied Carpet Beetle. This is an attractive insect and only tiny, around three millimetres long. There were a number of them on my Wild Carrot in 2012, which with luck will not lead to problems indoors.

Weevils often come in for criticism because of the damage they can do to crops and garden plants. The larvae generally live inside plant tissue while the adults attack the outside. In fact, only a relatively small proportion of the close to 600 species in Britain have any great impact on human activity. Some of them have stunning colouring, including the bright red Oak Roller Weevil, which as the name suggests makes containers for its brood principally on Oaks but also uses Sweet Chestnut among other trees. This species has been spotted in the garden on only one occasion, and it is fair to say once seen, never forgotten.

The Common Malachite looks spectacular when taking off

Two ground beetles, sizeable and fast-moving predators with attractive colouring. The Violet Ground Beetle (above left) turns up most years and the subtle livery is always a pleasure to see. The European Ground Beetle (above right) with its bronzy sheen is equally bonny but locally less common

The scarce Fungus weevil *Platystomos albinus*, photographed on a piece of dead wood near the greenhouse in 2009, is another striking member of the family, albeit not because of any gaudy colours. Their larvae feed on dead wood and the distinctly white markings set them apart from the vast majority of our invertebrates. One weevil that appeared on a Sweet Pea plant in 2012 is the Hazelnut Weevil, a fairly common species that burrows into the nuts with its long snout or rostrum and lays eggs there. In all probability this one had strayed in from the park where there are Hazel trees though most of the nuts they produce are eaten by Grey Squirrels every year. As one of the so-called 'True Weevils' the Hazelnut Weevil has geniculate or elbowed antennae on the rostrum.

A couple of soldier beetles, the black and red *Cantharis rustica* (left) and *Cantharis decipiens* (below)

Weevils can vary dramatically in colour, as this trio shows. They are an Oak Roller Weevil (below), a Hazelnut Weevil (above) and the fungus weevil *Platystomos albinus* (left)

213

Three species of beetle which, rightly or wrongly, are not popular in the 21st century. Top, an Oak Jewel Beetle; left, a Varied Carpet Beetle; below, a Rosemary Beetle

The leaf beetle *Gastrophysa polygoni*

SPECIES OF LADYBIRD RECORDED

Cream-streaked Ladybird *Harmonia 4-punctata*
Cream-spot Ladybird *Calvia 14-guttata*
Fourteen-spot Ladybird *Propylea 14-punctata*
Harlequin Ladybird *Harmonia axyridis*
Pine Ladybird *Exochomus 4-pustulatus*
Seven-spot Ladybird *Coccinella 7-punctata*
Twenty-two-spot Ladybird *Psyllobora 22-punctata*
Twenty-four-spot Ladybird *Subcoccinella 24-punctata*
Two-spot Ladybird *Adalia 2-punctata*

OTHER SPECIES OF BEETLE RECORDED

Bark beetle *Platypus cylindricus*
Black and Yellow Longhorn Beetle *Rutpela maculata*
Black-headed Cardinal Beetle *Pyrochroa coccinea*
Cockchafer *Melolontha melolontha*
Common Malachite *Malachius bipustulatus*
European Ground Beetle *Carabus nemoralis*
Fairy-ring Longhorn Beetle *Pseudovadonia livida*
Fungus weevil *Platystomos albinus*
Garden Chafer *Phyllopertha horticola*
Hazelnut Weevil *Curculio nucum*
Leaf beetle *Gastrophysa polygoni*
Lesser Stag Beetle *Dorcus parallelipipedus*
Oak Jewel Beetle *Agrilus biguttatus*
Oak Roller Weevil *Attelabus nitens*
Red-headed Cardinal Beetle *Pyrochroa serraticornis*

Rhinoceros Beetle *Sinodendron cylindricum*
Rosemary Beetle *Chrysolina americana*
Soldier beetle *Cantharis decipiens*
Soldier beetle *Cantharis rustica*
Speckled Longhorn Beetle *Pachytodes cerambyciformis*
Spruce Shortwing Longhorn Beetle *Molorchus minor*
Stag Beetle *Lucanus cervus*
Summer Chafer *Amphimallon solstitialis*
Swollen-thighed Beetle *Oedemera nobilis*
Tanner Beetle *Prionus coriarius*
Two-banded Longhorn Beetle *Rhagium bifasciatum*
Varied Carpet Beetle *Anthrenus verbasci*
Violet Ground Beetle *Carabus violaceus*
Wasp Beetle *Clytus arietis*

Chapter 10
Other Invertebrates

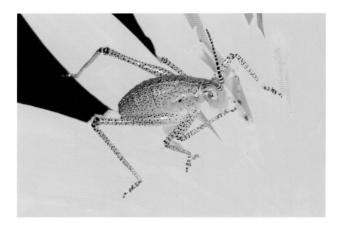

An immature Speckled Bush-cricket, and an
adult near the top of a Canadian Goldenrod
showing the considerable length of the antennae

Even after five chapters putting different insect families in the spotlight there are plenty of invertebrates left to report on, led by grasshoppers and bush-crickets (Orthoptera), bugs (Hemiptera) and spiders (Arachnida). The surrounding area is pretty thin on grasshoppers these days and after having plenty in the garden in 1964 only one species is regular now, the Field Grasshopper. Even that one, found mainly in the front garden each year, has taken something of a dive recently. They are exceptional fliers that can take to the air for up to 50 metres and their colour is variable, with individuals showing straw, buff, brown, green, purple or black.

The Field Grasshopper is herbivorous, as is the Speckled Bush-cricket, one of three types of bush-cricket seen on the premises. Bush-crickets tend to be bulkier than grasshoppers and their antennae are much longer. The Speckled bush-cricket is flightless and usually lurks among green vegetation where the colouring provides exceptional camouflage. The speckling on immatures is particularly noticeable. Dark Bush-crickets are omnivorous and have been seen only a couple of times while the Oak Bush-cricket is a carnivore, using powerful mouth parts to prey on small invertebrates. They live on various trees, not just Oak, and are often attracted into rooms with lights on and windows open. This is usually on warm nights in August – bush-crickets, in contrast to grasshoppers, are often active in the dark – and on one occasion in 2004 five Oak Bush-crickets were found on the walls and ceiling in the kitchen. Catching them to put them outside was no easy matter since they are strong fliers.

Moving on to bugs, the most obvious and frankly endearing of the tribe are shieldbugs and their allies, 14 of which have been noted in the garden, often visiting flowers but in several cases breeding. Their appeal is partly down to their variety of bright colouration but also to the apparently clumsy way virtually all of them fly, land and often move, especially

Female Dark Bush-cricket, with the scimitar-like ovipositor that characterises the family

Male Oak Bush-cricket on my bedroom curtain, a regular event on warm evenings a decade ago but not nowadays

Two contrasting colour forms of the Field Grasshopper, black and green, with the latter showing the typically reddish upper side to the abdomen

when dropping post haste out of sight off foliage when disturbed. Some species are predators, some are not.

The most interesting in the garden is the Box Bug. Box does well on nutrient poor soils including sand and the garden has one large and several small bushes which attract plenty of invertebrates. As the name suggests, the Box Bug has always used the plant, and until the late 1980s was restricted in range locally to Box Hill. However, the bug now also uses Hawthorn, Rose, Yew and even Apple and has begun to spread. To some extent this may be another indication of the benefits of warmer climatic conditions for certain invertebrate species, but either way Box Bugs have bred in

A Hawthorn Shieldbug, the largest of the family in Britain at 15 millimetres

Any runway will do – a Forest Bug after landing on my tripod by a bee box near the greenhouse in 2012

the garden regularly since 2000 and may be seen in almost any month from March to October, with a peak in late summer.

The Juniper Shieldbug has proved equally adaptable, as indeed it had to in order to survive locally. The original food plant of the species, Juniper, is in increasingly short supply in lowland England but the bug has taken to using Lawson's Cypress which, unlike the related and villainous Leyland Cypress, produces the cones the shieldbug requires. There is a Lawson's Cypress on a neighbour's property and clearly Juniper Bugs use this since they turn up in my garden most years.

The commonest shieldbug in the average Surrey garden and most other places nowadays is the Green Shieldbug but this one was far less easy to find in the 19th century, with only four sites listed in the Victoria County History as holding it. Green Shieldbugs benefit from being able to use a wide range of food plants, including runner beans. Like others in the family they hibernate, turning darker in colour before they do so. They reappear in April to start the next generation.

Another species which definitely has bred in the garden is the Hawthorn Shieldbug, the

Gorse Shieldbug getting ready for winter, with the coat changing colour and becoming brighter

A Green Shieldbug, the commonest species in the garden. They turn brown in autumn and hibernate among dead leaves

Juniper Bug (above) on Lawson's Cypress foliage

Tortoise Bugs are much less angular and more rotund than many of the family

Woundwort Bugs can be obvious one year then go missing for several. They are often found mating

largest in Britain at 15 millimetres and one of the most colourful. This species predictably has Hawthorn as the main food plant but also uses Whitebeam, Rowan and, crucially, Cotoneaster – it has bred on this plant in the back border. Also seen in the garden regularly, though never in large numbers, are the Forest Bug, found principally on Oak, and the Sloe Bug, which despite the name is not a specialist feeder. The latter is also known as the Hairy Shieldbug and a picture of a pair mating opens this chapter. The Dock Bug breeds mainly on docks and sorrels and is one of the commonest of all the group although it is not a genuine shieldbug. The robust antennae with four segments place it among the Coreidae or Squash Bug family, which also contains the Box Bug.

Less frequent visitors are the Parent Bug and the Gorse Shieldbug; the latter, like the Dock Bug, breeds in the disused sandpit over the road. The Parent Bug uses Birch or Alder trees and uniquely the female sits over her eggs and youngest nymphs, protecting them from predators and parasites. Like all but a handful in the family, the Gorse Shieldbug

Two predators which have appeared once in the garden – the tiny Blue Shieldbug and the larger Bronze Shieldbug

hibernates as an adult in any safe spot, be it in an evergreen, leaf litter or a cavity in wood. Unlike the majority, its colouring becomes brighter rather than duller in autumn, with definite red and blue tinges as opposed to green in the summer. Hibernation can make species vulnerable to bad weather – the Forest Bug, for instance, is one of only two species that hibernate as nymphs, staying high up in trees.

Two species, both predators, have turned up only once. The tiny Blue Shieldbug, which changes from red to blue as the nymph becomes an adult, appeared in 2006. This is not a common species and is as snappy in action as in appearance, preying on leaf beetles (*Altica* species) as both larvae and adults. *Troilus luridus*, which has only recently been given the

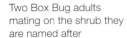

Two Box Bug adults mating on the shrub they are named after

English name Bronze Shieldbug, is brightly coloured as a youngster but much drabber when mature. They are fairly common and equally at home in broad-leaved and coniferous woodland, catching principally leaf beetles although prey as tough as ladybirds can be taken.

A couple of bugs from other families are worth mentioning. The capsid bug *Heterotoma planicornis* has bright green legs but even more distinctive are the antennae, which are decidedly thick and elongated. This is a common species, though I had never seen one in the garden until July 2012 on Great Willowherb. They feed on small invertebrates as well as plants. The plant bug *Leptopterna ferrugata* is also quite common, eating grasses.

Three insects described as flies which are not from the basic fly family, Diptera, merit a mention because of their looks and their behaviour. They are the Scorpion Fly *Panorpa communis* and the snakeflies *Atlantoraphidia maculicollis* and *Phaeostigma notata*. The male of

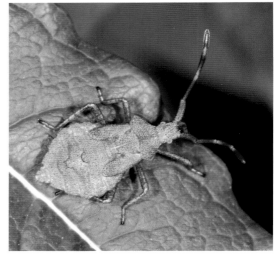

Dock Bug, from the same Coreidae family as Box Bugs

Snakeflies have turned up only in the gazebo. The female *Atlantoraphidia maculicollis* (below) shows the long ovipositor used to lay eggs in dead wood, while the elongate pronotum is evident in the male *Phaeostigma notata* (right)

Capsid bug *Heterotoma planicornis*, with the remarkable antennae in evidence

Green or bluish Lacewings like *Chrysoperla carnea* (above left) are the ones we see most often but there are others such as the Brown Lacewing *Micromus variegatus*, photographed on a home-grown lettuce

the former has the end of the abdomen curled for use in courtship, not hunting, and the species will feed on almost anything from rotting fruit to bird droppings. They are weak fliers, prefer shade to sun and can be easy to see, qualities they hold in common with their relatives, those apparently flimsy but marvellously elegant insects lacewings, which are voracious eaters of aphids and used to be seen regularly inside the house and out, though not so much recently. Green lacewings, usually of indeterminate species, have been the norm but my first sighting of the Brown Lacewing *Micromus variegatus* with its attractively marked wings was when I spotted one on a lettuce brought in from the vegetable plot in 2012.

Male Scorpion Fly on Holly, with the curled end to the abdomen visible

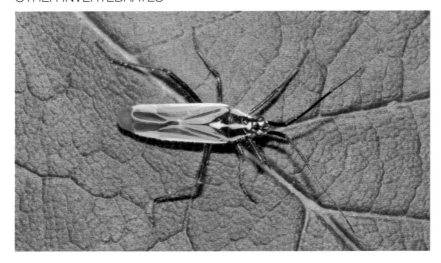

Male *Leptopterna ferrugata*, a relatively common bug. Males are fully winged, females only partly winged

Scorpion Flies are Mecoptera, lacewings are Neuroptera and snakeflies are Raphidioptera. The English name of the last-named comes from the length of the pronotum (like a neck) and the female uses her long ovipositor to lay eggs in the bark of dead or decaying trees, where the larvae dine on soft-bodied invertebrate larvae. There are only four species of snakefly in Britain, none of them that common, so it is remarkable to have had two in the garden, more specifically in the gazebo. I have never seen them anywhere else in the locale. *Atlantoraphidia maculicollis* uses Pine or Larch trees and *Phaeostigma notata* is found only around Oaks. Adult snakeflies eat aphids.

Heather with masses of spiders' webs visible after a relatively cool night in late August 2011

Spiders

There are around 600 species of spider in Britain and the vast majority are unknown to all but a few experts, partly because many hunt at night. Spiders are not popular even though they catch a host of invertebrates that are viewed as pests, and provide food for birds along with nest-building substances via their webs. Some research suggests that in western societies as many as 55 per cent of women and 18 per cent of men admit to experiencing arachnophobia. In my early teens I was not terribly keen whenever a House Spider arrived in the bath, or when one careered across the carpet in the front room, often pursued half-heartedly by the cat.

That feeling hardly amounted to arachnophobia though, and with age and increased understanding of how varied and fascinating they are, spiders have grown on me in a manner of speaking. In many respects spiders find their own niche inside or outside any property, large or small. This may be on internal walls, in cupboards or lofts, in garages, on cars, among roof tiles or on fascia boards, underneath plant pots, in piles of logs, stones or bricks, in greenhouses, sheds or nest boxes, on trees, shrubs or smaller plants, on the lawn…the list is almost endless and so are the numbers of spiders, as a morning dew in late summer often reveals. If a gardener provides habitats for other forms of wildlife, spiders normally will be able to take full advantage.

There are no claims to have identified more than a small proportion of the spiders that inhabit my garden and house, and I am grateful to Peter Harvey of the British Arachnological Society for providing assistance with a number of those that have been confirmed. Starting inside the house, it is sad to report that House Spiders appear much less regularly than they did 20 years ago. There was a male in the bath in October 2012 but the best place for them nowadays is in detritus lying on the floor of the greenhouse, such as wooden slats and plant pots – it always pays to be careful when shifting anything in such

Zilla diodia with a fly much larger than herself

locations. Most of the House Spiders seen are males but there is no certainty of the species since there are six different ones in the *Tegenaria* genus.

Daddy Long-legs Spiders are frequently found inside houses and outhouses and their cobwebs can be a seemingly perpetual source of annoyance to those wielding dusters. I am pretty relaxed about them and enjoy watching their antics, including when one caught quite a large spider of a different genus near the skirting board in the front room. Another memorable sight, though my parents were less

The Common Fox-spider pictured on the doormat almost certainly was brought in by one of the family after a bout of gardening. They do not live inside properties, unlike Daddy Long-legs Spiders, which are unwelcome to most people because of the cobwebs they habitually create to snare prey. In the mid-1990s the pictured female had numerous offspring in the section containing the boiler. Opposite, House Spiders, including males in the bath, are also none too popular. They are found in the garage, sheds and greenhouse too, and in 2012 a *Stelis breviuscula* bee fell foul of a young male lurking in a bamboo cane

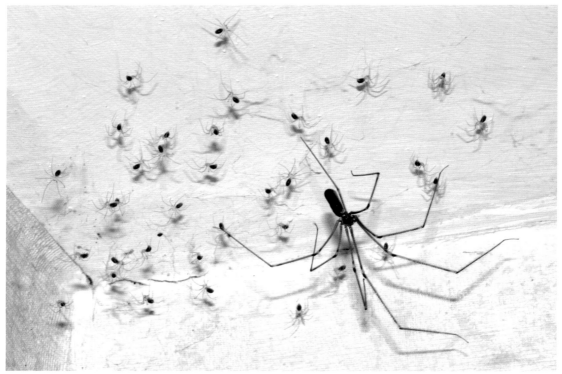

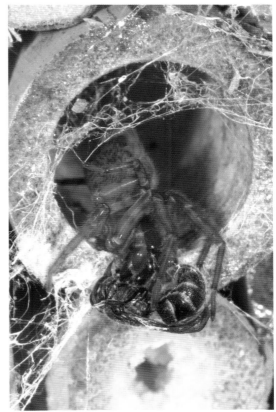

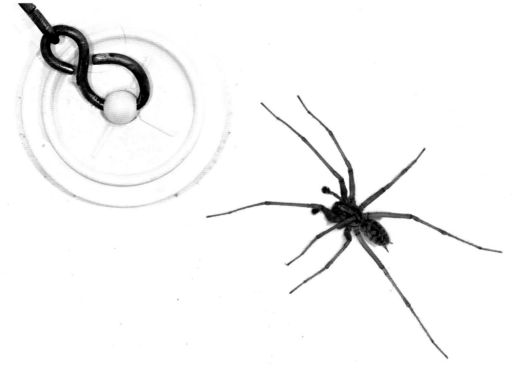

Garden Spiders make hay catching almost anything that gets trapped in their beautiful but deadly webs, including as here a Seven-spot Ladybird. The colouring can be quite bright, as with a red version who set up her web on Heather in 2012. Large groups of spiderlings are to be seen most years. If touched, they separate rapidly but they remain vulnerable to some predators such as *Trypoxylon* solitary wasps

Crab spiders are powerful and hunt on foot, not using a web. Remember the image on page 20? The inappropriate yellow hue of the *Misumena vatia* did not prevent her catching a large fly for sustenance (left), any more than the white colour of another hindered her in catching a Garden Chafer beetle. The other species shown is the common *Xysticus cristatus* on a Forget-Me-Not flower

Araniella species can be fairly colourful; this is a male, almost certainly *Araniella cucurbitina*

impressed, was a brood of juveniles with their mother on a wall near the boiler in the kitchen. Other spiders appear indoors, some of them nocturnal hunters that are in their correct niche but others by mistake. The latter group included a Comb-footed Spider, a sometimes colourful species with long legs that uses a web to catch quite large prey, and a wolf spider called the Common Fox-spider, which occupies open habitats of all kinds so was a bit out of place on the front doormat.

Moving outside, the best-known spider is the Garden Spider or Cross Spider. The latter title is based on the markings on the back of the abdomen, which is generally but not always brown or fawn. A bright red one on Heather in 2012 was a revelation, though I had seen them with this colouring several times elsewhere. With their superbly constructed circular webs and their bulk, especially in

autumn, Garden Spiders are familiar to everyone and they are adaptable, in so far as two females nested in successive years in the greenhouse. This made good sense, given the number of quite large invertebrates that went in there by accident or design, including bumblebees for the tomato flowers, and social wasps. The Ivy and Heather in the garden are also favoured spots because of the number of bees that frequent the blooms to collect pollen. Wasps are fair game too, but the boot can sometimes be on the other foot since some skilled Common Wasps or German Wasps occasionally work out that harrying and buzzing a Garden Spider mercilessly while staying just out of range can result in free access to captured prey as the host takes refuge on the margin of the web.

Some spider species carry their young on the back but not the Garden Spider, which can

Jumping spiders are quite small and chunky with two large eyes at the front that afford good binocular vision. They are frequently seen, especially the Zebra Spider (1), which can jump more than ten centimetres (four inches) to take prey. *Marpissa muscosa* (2) is a bit bigger and less common. *Sitticus pubescens* (3), *Evarcha falcata* (male, 4) and *Heliophanus flavipes* (5) have been seen only occasionally

The Woodlouse Spider can give humans quite a painful nip

This Common False-widow Spider caught both solitary bees and solitary wasps after setting up her web on dead wood near the greenhouse. The pictured victim is the wasp *Crossocerus annulipes*

have dozens of progeny which are guarded closely once they change from larvae to mobile nymphs or spiderlings. A much smaller orb-web spider, one whose web is less perfect to human eyes because seemingly rather ragged with a lot of radii, is *Zilla diodia*. Females are just four millimetres in length and the species was formerly nationally scarce, so it was good to see one using a Box bush for her web in May 2012. She caught a fly vastly bigger than she was, so ragged or not, the web clearly was effective. The Box is also a regular haunt of the pretty little green-coloured orb-web spider *Araniella cucurbitina*.

Camouflage is extremely useful for many predators as well as prey and spiders make full use of this. The most conspicuous example is the relatively rotund crab spider *Misumena vatia*. The spread of the legs explains the English name and these spiders are common in almost every habitat including gardens. They have a tremendous advantage in being able to change colour to suit whichever plant they are living on, lying in wait on or underneath flowers for potential prey seeking nectar. The range covers white, yellow or green and everything in between, and this enables them to get close to and seize prey up to the size of bumblebees. The majority of the flowers in my borders are yellow or white,

Female *Pardosa* species wolf spiders carry their eggs in a sac under the body. After hatching, the young ride on the mother's back for a week or so. In 2010 one of my bee boxes provided a good shelter for the pictured female with her sac alongside a closed Red Mason Bee nest. Below, a Walnut Orb-weaver Spider used another of the cardboard tubes later the same year

which makes them prime territory for *Misumena vatia*, and they do pretty well.

Stalking is not frenetic but is undoubtedly effective and the only failure (that I have seen) to take prey ranging from flies to bees via earwigs occurred when the legs of what was a small specimen proved unable to grip a male mason bee. Whether the camouflage is designed to protect the spider from predators, or conceal her presence from her own intended prey items, is a moot point. White- and yellow-coloured *Misumena vatia* have twice been on Californian Lilac, which has blue flowers, but in 2012 a yellow one caught a large fly despite sticking out like a sore thumb. *Misumena vatia* hunts on foot as does the long-legged Nursery Web Spider, which tends to lurk in vegetation in the borders but enjoys sunbathing.

The most productive area for spiders is where dead wood and boxes have been inserted for bees and wasps. The logs are ideal for the Woodlouse Spider, which preys only on woodlice and can sometimes be found beneath

Nursery Web Spiders enjoy basking on sunlit leaves and can be seen most years. This is a female

Not a pretty sight for most people, especially gardeners, but the Common Garden Slug *Arion distinctus* (below) can do a lot of good work eating decaying vegetable matter and algae to compensate for its less acceptable activities

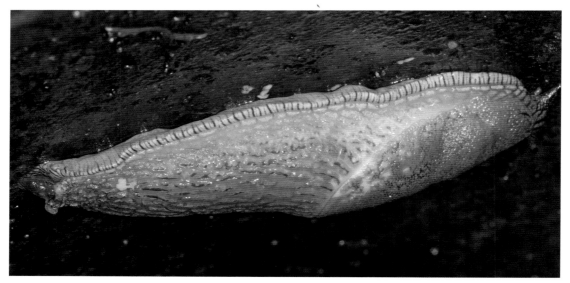

plant pots and bins. Invertebrate nesting areas are an open invitation for predators to set up home and Common False-widow Spiders build webs on logs most years. One female did particularly well in 2008, catching several *Crossocerus annulipes* digger wasps that were nesting in the logs. The bonny and plentiful Zebra Spider, a jumping spider, also uses the boxes as a hunting ground. Others of that ilk to have been seen on the wood include *Sitticus*

pubescens and the nationally scarce *Marpissa muscosa*, which has also been present in the adjacent greenhouse.

Two other jumping spiders have been noted on the logs, *Evarcha falcata* and *Heliophanus flavipes* – *Heliophanus* species are a favoured prey of the spider-hunting wasp *Agenioideus cinctellus*. The holes in the insect boxes provide shelter for a number of species, notably the fairly sizeable Walnut Orb-weaver Spider, a

Garden Snails are hermaphrodites but they can engage in courtship and mating

This Brown-lipped Snail (left) has numerous marks on the shell, indicating that it is probably several years old.

nocturnal species that has quite a painful bite. In 2010, a *Pardosa* wolf spider with her egg sac characteristically attached to the abdomen spent more than a week around one box, including occupying a cardboard tube alongside one that had been stocked by a Red Mason Bee. An immature male House Spider living in a bamboo cane in a box caught a female *Stelis breviuscula* cuckoo bee in 2012.

The last word on invertebrates goes to a family that most gardeners see as the clear-cut enemy: slugs and snails. They eat some of the bedding plants, vegetables and salad leaves, and they get into greenhouses, outhouses and the house itself on occasions. Even if pellets are

SPECIES OF GRASSHOPPER AND CRICKET RECORDED

Dark Bush-cricket *Pholidoptera griseoaptera*
Field Grasshopper *Chorthippus brunneus*

Oak Bush-cricket *Meconema thalassinum*
Speckled Bush-cricket *Leptophyes punctatissima*

SPECIES OF SHIELDBUG RECORDED

Blue Shieldbug *Zicrona caerulea*
Box Bug *Gonocerus acuteangulatus*
Brassica Bug *Eurydema oleracea*
Bronze Shieldbug *Troilus luridus*
Dock Bug *Coreus marginatus*
Forest Bug *Pentatoma rufipes*
Gorse Shieldbug *Piezodorus lituratus*
Green Shieldbug *Palomena prasina*
Hawthorn Shieldbug *Acanthosoma haemorrhoidale*
Juniper Shieldbug *Cyphostethus tristriatus*
Parent Bug *Elasmucha grisea*
Sloe Bug *Dolycoris baccarum*
Tortoise Bug *Eurygaster testudinaria*
Woundwort Bug *Eysarcoris fabricii*

SPECIES OF SPIDER RECORDED

Common False-widow Spider *Steatoda bipunctata*
Common Fox-spider *Alopecosa pulverulenta*
Comb-footed Spider *Enoplognatha ovata*
Crab spider *Misumena vatia*
Crab spider *Xysticus cristatus*
Daddy Long-legs Spider *Pholcus phalangioides*
Garden Spider *Araneus diadematus*
House Spider *Tegenaria sp*
Jumping spider *Evarcha falcata*
Jumping spider *Heliophanus flavipes*
Jumping spider *Marpissa muscosa*
Jumping spider *Sitticus pubescens*
Nursery Web Spider *Pisaura mirabilis*
Orb-web spider *Araniella cucurbitina*
Orb-web spider *Zilla diodia*
Walnut Orb-weaver Spider *Nuctenea umbratica*
Wolf spider *Pardosa sp*
Woodlouse Spider *Dysdera crocata*
Zebra Spider *Salticus scenicus*

used – an understandable but hardly environmentally friendly method of control – they keep coming back for more, with the garden hosting hundreds if not thousands each year. Birds, led by Song Thrushes but also including Jackdaws, Magpies, Robins and Blackbirds, prey on them while frogs, toads and newts eat a proportion of slugs.

The attentions of these predators have some effect but arguably not a dramatic one. The fact that a Garden Snail *Helix aspera* can have more than 400 progeny in a year may help explain this, as may the fact that snails (slugs too) are hermaphrodites, with both male and female reproductive organs. The Garden Snail and the Brown-lipped Snail *Cepaea nemoralis* are the commonest of the band and are long-lived

given the chance, seven or eight years sometimes. Wet conditions suit snails very well but if there is a prolonged dry spell they seal the shell and engage in what amounts to suspended animation.

Some Brown-lipped Snails (opposite) show wonderfully dashing colours, such as this one at the top of a cane used to support a Canterbury-bell plant

Bibliography

Asher, J., Warren, M., Fox, R., Harding, P., Jeffcoate, G. and Jeffcoate, S. 2001. The Millennium Atlas of Butterflies in Britain and Ireland. Oxford University Press, Oxford.

Baines, C. 2000. How to Make a Wildlife Garden. Frances Lincoln Ltd, London.

Baldock, D. W. 1999. Grasshoppers and Crickets of Surrey. Surrey Wildlife Trust, Woking.

Baldock, D. W. 2008. Bees of Surrey. Surrey Wildlife Trust, Woking.

Baldock, D. W. 2010. Wasps of Surrey. Surrey Wildlife Trust, Woking.

Ball, S. and Morris, R. 2013. Britain's Hoverflies – An introduction to the hoverflies of Britain. Princeton University Press, New Jersey.

Blamey, M., Fitter, R. and Fitter, A. 2003. Wild Flowers of Britain and Ireland. A. & C. Black, London.

British Dragonfly Society. 1996. Dig a Pond for Dragonflies. British Dragonfly Society.

Brooks, S. J. and Lewington, R. 1997. Field Guide to the Dragonflies and Damselflies of Great Britain and Ireland. British Wildlife Publishing, Hook.

Bucknill, J. A. 1900. The Birds of Surrey. R. H. Porter, London.

Buczacki, S. 2002. Fauna Britannica. Hamlyn, London.

Buczacki, S. 2007. Garden Natural History, Collins New Naturalist Library. Harper Collins, London.

Carter, D. J. and Hargreaves, B. 1986. A Field Guide to the Caterpillars of Butterflies & Moths in Britain and Europe. Collins, London.

Chinery, M. 1973. A Field Guide to the Insects of Britain and Western Europe. Collins, London.

Chinery, M. 1986. Collins Guide to the Insects of Britain and Western Europe. Harper Collins, London.

Chinery, M. 1999. Garden Wildlife of Britain and Europe, Collins Nature Guides. Harper Collins, London.

Chinery, M. 2004. Attracting Wildlife to Your Garden. Harper Collins, London.

Clark, M. 2010. Badgers. Whittet Books, Suffolk.

Clements, D. K. 1997. The Enemy Within: Conopid flies as parasitoids of bees and wasps in Britain. British Wildlife 8 (5): 310-315.

Cocker, M. and Mabey, R. 2005. Birds Britannica. Random House UK, London.

Collins, G. A. 1995. Butterflies of Surrey. Surrey Wildlife Trust, Woking.

Collins, G. A. 1997. Larger Moths of Surrey. Surrey Wildlife Trust, Woking.

Corbet, P. S. 1999. Dragonflies: Behaviour and Ecology of Odonata. Harley Books, Colchester.

Cramp, S. et al. 1977-1994. The Handbook of the Birds of Europe, North Africa and the Middle East, 1-9. Oxford University Press, Oxford.

Day, M. C. 1988. Spider Wasps (Hymenoptera: Pompilidae). Handbooks for the Identification of British Insects. 6, Part 4. Royal Entomological Society, London.

Denton, J. 2005. The Beetles of Surrey: A Checklist. Surrey Wildlife Trust, Woking.

Denton, J. 2007. Water Bugs and Water Beetles of Surrey. Surrey Wildlife Trust, Woking.

Drewett, J. 1987. The Nature of Surrey. Barracuda Books Ltd, Buckingham.

Edwards, M. and Jenner, M. 2005. Field Guide to the Bumblebees of Great Britain and Ireland. Ocelli Publishing Ltd, Eastbourne.

Else, G.R. 1999. Identification – Leaf-cutter Bees. British Wildlife 10 (6): 388-393.

Else, G.R. In prep. Handbook of the bees of the British Isles.

Falk, S. J. 1991. A review of the scarce and threatened bees, wasps and ants of Great Britain. Research and Survey in Nature Conservation, 35. Nature Conservancy Council, Peterborough.

Falk, S. J. 1991. A review of the scarce and threatened flies of Great Britain (part 1). Research and Survey in Nature Conservation, 39. Nature Conservancy Council, Peterborough.

Fitter, R. and Manuel, R. 1986. Collins Field Guide to Freshwater Life. Collins, London.

Follett, P. 1996. Dragonflies of Surrey. Surrey Wildlife Trust, Woking.

Forsythe, T. G. 1987. Common Ground Beetles. Richmond Publishing Co., Slough.

Fox, R., Conrad, K., Parsons, M., Warren, M. and Woiwod, I. 2006. The State of Britain's Larger Moths. Butterfly Conservation & Rothamsted Research.

Gibbons, B. and Gibbons, L. 1992. Creating a Wildlife Garden. Hamlyn, London.

Guthrie, M. 1989. Animals on the surface film. Richmond Publishing Co., Slough.

Harde, K. W. 1999. Field Guide in Colour to Beetles. Blitz Editions, Leicester.

Harris, S. and Baker, P. 2001. Urban Foxes. Whittet Books, Suffolk.

Hawkins, R. D. 2000. Ladybirds of Surrey. Surrey Wildlife Trust, Woking.

Hawkins, R. D. 2003. Shieldbugs of Surrey. Surrey Wildlife Trust, Woking.

Holloway, S. 1996. The Historical Atlas of Breeding Birds in Britain and Ireland, 1875-1900. T. & A. D. Poyser, London.

Hymm, P. S. and Parsons, M. S. 1992. A review of the scarce and threatened Coleoptera of Great Britain (part 1). U. K. Nature Conservation, 3. Joint Nature Conservation Committee, Peterborough.

Jones, D. 1983. The Country Life Guide to Spiders of Britain and Northern Europe. Country Life Books, Middlesex.

Kerney, M. P. and Cameron, R. A. D. 1979. The Land Snails of Britain and North-west Europe. Collins, London.

Leather, S. R. and Bland, K. P. 1999. Insects on cherry trees. Richmond Publishing Co., Slough.

Lewington, R. 2008. Guide to Garden Wildlife. British Wildlife Publishing, Dorset.

Little, M. 2012. Plants and Planting Plans for a Bee Garden: How to Design Beautiful Borders That Will Attract Bees. Spring Hill, Oxford.

Lomholdt, O. 1975. The Sphecidae (Hymenoptera) of Fennoscandia and Denmark. Fauna Entomologica Scandinavica 4.

Lousley, J. E. 1976. Flora of Surrey. David & Charles, Newton Abbot.

Mabey, R. 1998. Flora Britannica. Chatto & Windus, London.

Macdonald, D. and Barrett, P. 1993. Field Guide to the Mammals of Britain & Europe. Harper Collins, London.

Majerus, M and Kearns, P. 1989. Ladybirds. Richmond Publishing Co., Slough.

Malden, H. E. ed. 1902. The Victoria county history of Surrey, 1. Westminster, London.

Marren, P. 2010. Bugs Britannica. Chatto & Windus, London.

Marshall, J. A. and Haes E. C. M. 1988. Grasshoppers and Allied Insects of Great Britain and Ireland. Harley Books, Colchester.

Michener, C. D. 2000. The Bees of the World. John Hopkins University Press, Baltimore.

Morgan, D. 1984. Cuckoo wasps (Hymenoptera, Chrysididae). Handbooks for the Identification of British Insects. 6, Part 5. Royal Entomological Society, London.

Morris, P. 2010. The New Hedgehog Book. Whittet Books, Suffolk.

Morris, R. K. A. 1998. Hoverflies of Surrey. Surrey Wildlife Trust, Woking.

Neal, E. and Cheeseman, C. 1996. Badgers. T. & A. D. Poyser, London.

O'Toole, C. 2002. Bumblebees: their natural history and how to attract them to the garden. Osmia Publications, Banbury.

O'Toole, C. and Raw, A. 1991. Bees of the World. Blandford, London.

Owen, J. 2010. Wildlife of a Garden: A Thirty-Year Study. Royal Horticultural Society, London.

Palmer, R. M., Porter J. and Collins, G. A. 2012. Smaller Moths of Surrey. Surrey Wildlife Trust, Woking.

Parr, D. 1972. Birds in Surrey 1900-1970. Batsford, London.

Phillips, R. 1981. Mushrooms and Other Fungi of Great Britain and Europe. Pan Books, London.

Pontin, J. 2005. Ants of Surrey. Surrey Wildlife Trust, Woking.

Prys-Jones, O. E. and Corbet S. A. 1991. Bumblebees. Richmond Publishing Co., Slough.

Richards, O. W. 1980. Scolioidea, Vespoidea and Sphecoidea (Hymenoptera, Aculeata). Handbooks for the Identification of British Insects. 6. Part 3 (b). Royal Entomological Society, London.

Saunders, E. 1896. British Hymenoptera Aculeata. Reeve & Co, London.

Shirt, D.B. ed. 1987. Insects. British Red Data Books, 2. Nature Conservancy Council, Peterborough.

Simms, E. 1971. Woodland Birds. Collins, London.

Skinner, B. 1986. Colour Identification Guide to Moths of the British Isles. Viking, Middlesex.

Stace, C. 2010. New Flora of The British Isles. 3rd edition. Cambridge University Press, Cambridge.

Sterling, P., Parsons, M. and Lewington, R. 2012. Field Guide to the Micro-moths of Great Britain and Ireland. British Wildlife Publishing, Dorset.

Stubbs, A. E. and Drake, C. M. 2001. British Soldierflies and their Allies: A Field Guide to the Larger British Brachycera. British Entomological and Natural History Society, Reading.

Stubbs, A. E. and Falk, S. J. 2002. British Hoverflies. An Illustrated Identification Guide. 2nd edition. British Entomological and Natural History Society, Reading.

Thomas, A. 2010. RSPB Gardening for Wildlife – a Complete Guide to Nature-friendly Gardening. A. & C. Black, London.

Thomas, J. A. 1991. The Butterflies of Britain and Ireland. Dorling Kindersley, London.

Waring, P., Townsend, M. and Lewington, R. 2009. Field Guide to the Moths of Great Britain and Ireland. 2nd edition. British Wildlife Publishing, Dorset.

Wheatley, J. J. 2007. Birds of Surrey. Surrey Bird Club.

Wilson, M. 2011. Nature's Garden – How to Garden in the 21st Century. Mitchell Beazley, London.

Wiśniowski, B. 2009. Spider-hunting Wasps (Hymenoptera: Pompilidae) of Poland. Ojcow National Park, Poland.

Wright, W. 1990. British Sawflies. A key to adults of the genera occurring in Britain, Field Studies Council No. 203. Field Studies Council.

Wycherley, J. and Anstis, R. 2001. Amphibians and Reptiles of Surrey. Surrey Wildlife Trust, Woking.

Yeo, P. F. and Corbet, S. A. 1995. Solitary Wasps. 2nd edition. Richmond Publishing Co., Slough.

Websites

Bees, Wasps and Ants Recording Society
www.bwars.com

British Arachnological Society
www.britishspiders.org.uk

British Dragonfly Society
www.british-dragonflies.org.uk

British Trust for Ornithology www.bto.org

Buglife www.buglife.org.uk

Butterfly Conservation
www.butterfly-conservation.org including PDF The State of the UK's Butterflies 2011

David Element
www.david.element.ukgateway.net

Jeremy Early
www.natureconservationimaging.com

Plantlife www.plantlife.org.uk

Royal Society for the Protection of Birds
www.rspb.org.uk including PDF
Birds of conservation concern 3 2009

Steven Falk www.stevenfalk.co.uk

Surrey Wildlife Trust
www.surreywildlifetrust.org

Wildlife Gardening Forum
www.naturalengland.org.uk/advice/wildlifegardening/forum.aspx

Bold denotes an image.
English and scientific names are given for every species that has both.

Acanthosoma haemorrhoidale **220**, 221, 238
Accipiter nisus **60**, 61, **61**, 64, 81
Acer platanoides 14, 24, 64, 84
Achillea millefolium 22, 24, 148
Acronicta aceris **115**, 115
Adalia 2-punctata 200, 201, **204**, 215
Adela reaumurella 115
Aegithalos caudatus **72**, 80, 81
Aesculus hipposcastanum 19, 24, 220, 222
Aeshna cyanea 54, 87, **88**, 89, 93
Aeshna grandis 88, 93
Aeshna mixta 88, **89**, 93
Agenioideus cinctellus **149**, 155, 170, 236
Aglais urticae 97, 98, 101, **104**, 114
Aglossa pinguinalis 111, **112**, 115
Agrilus biguttatus 204, **214**, 215
Alder 222
Alderfly **90**, 91, 93
Alectoris rufa **64**, 81
Alkanet, Green 22, 24
Alopecosa pulverulenta **228**, 232, 238
Amphimallon solstitialis 207, **210**, 215
Anas platyrhynchos 63, 81
Ancistrocerus gazella 40, **40**, 170
Ancistrocerus nigricornis 149, **152-3**, **154**, 157-9, 170
Ancistrocerus trifasciatus 149, **153**, 157-9, 170
Andrena argentata 121, 141
Andrena barbilabris 141
Andrena bicolor 141
Andrena dorsata 135, 141
Andrena flavipes 30, **30**, 121, 141
Andrena florea 135, 141
Andrena fulva 18, **121**, 122, 141
Andrena fuscipes 141
Andrena haemorrhoa **14**, 135, 141
Andrena labialis **122**, 141
Andrena labiata **15**, 32, **32**, 138, 141
Andrena minutula 14, **15**, 121, 141
Andrena nigroaenea 121, **121**
Andrena nitida 135, 141
Andrena semilaevis 141
Andrena trimmerana 28, **29**, 141

Angle Shades **107**, 110, 115
Anoplius infuscatus **150**, 156, 170
Anoplius nigerrimus 40, **41**, **150**, 155, 170
Anthidium manicatum **116-7**, **136**, 137, 141
Anthocharis cardamines 96, **100**, 114
Anthophila fabriciana **112**, 115
Anthophora bimaculata **123**, 140, 141
Anthophora furcata 141
Anthophora plumipes **124**, 140, 141
Anthrenus verbasci 211, **214**, 215
Ants 63
Apis mellifera 118-20, **140**, 140
Apodemus sylvaticus 47, **53**, 54
Apple 14, **14**, 24, 105, 107, 113, **179**, **197**, 220
Apple Sawfly 170
Apple-leaf Skeletonizer **110**, 115
Arachnospila anceps **150**, 155, 170
Arachnospila spissa 170
Arachnospila trivialis 155, 170
Araneus diadematus 38, **39**, **230**, 232, 238
Araniella cucurbitina **232**, 234, 238
Ardea cinerea 81, 86, **92**
Arge berberidis **170**, 171
Arge pagana **169**, 171
Arge ustulata 171
Argogorytes mystaceus 32, **33**, **155**, 170
Argynnis aglaja 99, 114
Argynnis paphia 100, 114
Arion distinctus **236**, 237-8
Artogeia napi 32, **33**, **98**, 100, 114
Artogeia rapae 100, 114
Astata boops 36, **36**, 148, 162, 170
Aster novi-belgii 20, 24
Asteraceae 22, 25, 40, 120, 132, 181
Athalia rosae 171
Atlantoraphidia maculicollis **224**, 226
Attelabus nitens 211, **213**, 215
Auplopus carbonarius **151,** 155, 170
Autographa gamma 110, **113**, 115

Backswimmer 90, **91**, 93
Badger 46, **47**, **48**, 51-53, 54, 184
Bat, Pipistrelle 54
Bedstraw 110
Bee hotels **21**, **26**, 123-135, **137**
Beech 10, 122, 175, 203
Bees 116-141

Beetles 198-215
Beewolf 162, **164**,
Begonia 21, 24
Berberis Sawfly **170**,171
Bibio marci 195, 197, 197
Bidens 22, **23**, 24, 132, **135**, **175**
Bidens ferulifolia 22, **23**, 24, 132, **135**, **175**
Birch 107, 175, 203, 222
Bird's-foot-trefoil, Common 24, **25**, 99, 111
Birds 58-81
Black and Yellow Longhorn Beetle 203, **205**, 215
Blackbird **27**, **67**, 73, 74, 81, 238
Blackcap 81
Black-headed Cardinal Beetle 204, 215
Blackthorn 98
Blue Carpenter Bee **124**, 138
Blue Mason Bee **25**, 129, **129**
Blue Shieldbug 223, **223**, 238
Blue, Common 25, 99, 114
Blue, Holly 38, **38**, 96, **98**, 99, 114
Bluebell 19, 24
Bluebottle **190**
Bombus campestris **139**, 140
Bombus hortorum 15, **20**, 140
Bombus hypnorum 21, 105, 120, **138**, 140
Bombus lapidarius **18**, 120, 135, **138**, 140
Bombus lucorum 14, 30, 38, **39**, 140
Bombus pascuorum **20**, 28, **28**, 120, 135, 140
Bombus pratorum **19**, 120, **139**, 140
Bombus rupestris 136, **139**, 140
Bombus subterraneus 120
Bombus sylvestris 140
Bombus terrestris **18**, 30, 135, 140
Bombus vestalis 136, **139**, 140
Bombylius major 28, **29**, 188, **188**, 197
Box 19, 24, **111**, 191, 220, 234
Box Bug 220, 222, **223**, 238
Brachypalpoides lentus 175, **175**, 196
Bracken 19, 24
Bramble 18, 24, 99
Bramley's Seedling 14, 24, **178**
Brassica Bug 238
Brimstone 96, **96**, 114
British Dragonfly Society 60
Broad Centurion **189**, 190, 197
Bronze Shieldbug **223**, 224, 238

Broom 19, **19**, 24
Brown Lacewing 225, **225**
Brown, Meadow 100, **100**, 114
Brown-lipped Snail **237**, 238, **239**
Buckthorn 98
Buddleja 97, **185**
Buff-tailed Bumblebee **18**, 30, 135, 140
Bufo bufo 85, **86**, 93
Bullfinch **8**, 61, 62, **76**, 81
Bumblebees 118-20
Bunting, Corn 10
Burnet Companion 107, **111**, 115
Busy Lizzie 21
Butterflies 96-103
Butterfly Conservation 9, 60, 76, 97, 104
Buxus sempervirens 19, 24, **111**, 191, 220, 234
Buzzard 61

Caliadurgus fasciatellus 170
Callicera aurata 32, **33**, 174, **174**, 196
Calliphora vicina **190**
Calluna vulgaris 19, 24, 38, **38-9**, 105, **111**, **113**, **119**, 120, 139, **226**, 232
Caltha palustris 20, 24, 87
Calvia 14-guttata **200**, 215
Cameraria ohridella 113, 115
Campanula medium 19, **21**, 24, 34, **34-5**, **125**
Camptogramma bilineata 107, **115**, 115
Canterbury-bell 19, **21**, 24, 34, **34-5**, **125**
Cantharis decipiens **212**, 215
Cantharis rustica 210, **212**, 215
Capreolus capreolus 46, **46**, 51, 54
Carabus nemoralis **212**, 215
Carabus violaceus 209, **212**, 215
Carduelis carduelis 63, 81
Carduelis chloris 73, 74, **74**, 76, 81
Carduelis spinus **77**, 80, 81
Carrot, Wild 22, 24, 36, **36-7**, **136**, 148, **148**, **150**, **169**, **170**, 171, 178, **182**, 186, **193**, 194, 210, 211
Cat, domestic 47, 54, **54**, 61, 74
Cat's-ear 22, 24
Ceanothus **20**, 22, 24, 235
Celastrina argiolus 38, **38**, 96, **98**, 99, 114
Centaurea nigra 22, 24
Centaurea scabiosa 22, 24
Centroptilum luteolum 89, **91**, 93

Cepaea nemoralis **237**, 238, **239**
Ceratina cyanea **124**, 138, 141
Cerceris arenaria 162, **164**, 170
Cerceris rybyensis 38, **38**, 162, 171
Certhia familiaris 81
Chaenomeles japonica 20, 24
Chaffinch **75**, 74, 76, 81
Chalcid (wasp) **171**
Chamaecyparis lawsoniana 73, 84, 221
Charlock 100
Chaser, Broad-bodied 88, **88**, 93
Cheilosia caerulescens **175**, 183, 196
Cheilosia illustrata **176**, 183, 196
Cheilosia impressa 196
Cheilosia pagana 196
Cheilosia proxima 196
Cheilosia scutellata 196
Cheilosia soror 196
Cheilosia vernalis 196
Cheilosia vulpina 196
Chelostoma campanularum 34, **34**, 141
Chelostoma florisomne 141
Cherry Laurel 14, **15**, 24, 107, **178**, 202
Cherry, flowering 14, 24, 28, **28-9**, **183**
Chiffchaff 81
Chloromyia formosa **189**, 190, 197
Choreutis pariana **110**, 115
Chorthippus brunneus 219, **220**, 238
Chrysis angustula 170
Chrysis ignita **147**, 149, 170
Chrysis illigeri **147**, 149, 170
Chrysogaster solstitialis **186**, 196
Chrysolina americana 210, **214**, 215
Chrysoperla carnea **225**
Chrysotoxum bicinctum **180**, 181, 196
Chrysotoxum cautum **180**, 181, 196
Chrysotoxum festivum **180**, 181, 196
Cinnabar 107, **108**, 115
Cleg fly 189, **190**
Clepsis consimilana **111**, 115
Climate 22-23
Clover, White 22, 24, **25**
Clytus arietis 32, **33**, **198-9**, 215
Coccinella 7-punctata 28, **29**, 200, **201**, 215, **230**
Cockchafer 207, **209**, 215
Coelioxys elongata **135**, 136, 141
Coelioxys inermis 136, 141

Colletes hederae 42, **42**, **119**, 139, 141
Colletes succinctus 38, **39**, **118**, 136, 139, 141
Columba livia 66, 81
Columba palumbus 66, 73, 74, **77**, 81
Comb-footed Spider 232, 238
Comma 98, 99, 102, **102**, 114
Common Carder Bee **20**, 28, **28**, 120, 135, 140
Common Carpet 110, **111**, 115
Common False-widow Spider **234**, 236, 238
Common Fox-spider **228**, 232, 238
Common Malachite 210, **211**, 215
Common Nettle-tap **112**, 115
Common Wasp 28, **28**, 144, **145**, 170, 178, 232
Compost 185
Conopid flies 190-2
Conops ceriaeformis 192, **192**, 197
Conops quadrifasciatus 192, **192**, 197
Copper, Small 99, **100**, 114
Coreopsis grandiflora 22, 24
Coreus marginatus 222, **224**, 238
Corvus corone corone 66, **80**, 81, 195
Corvus frugilegus 81, 195
Corvus monedula **11**, 68, 70, **80**, 81, **81**, 238
Cossus cossus 178
Cotoneaster 19, **21**, 24, 105, **139**, 178, 222
Crab spiders **20**, **231**, 234, 238
Crab-apple 113
Crabro peltarius **156**, 171
Crambus lathoniellus **111**, 115
Crane's-bill 20, **23**, 24
Crane-fly 195, **196**, 197
Crataegus monogyna 19, 24, 220, 222
Cratichneumon species **166**
Cream-spot Ladybird **200**, 215
Cream-streaked Ladybird 200, **202**, 215
Criorhina floccosa 178, **178**, 196
Criorhina ranunculi 14, 175, **178**, 196
Crocus 19, 24, **140**
Crossocerus annulipes **156**, 160, 171, **234**
Crossocerus cetratus 171
Crossocerus distinguendus 171
Crossocerus megacephalus **156**, 159, 162, 171, 190
Crossocerus ovalis 171
Crossocerus podagricus 171
Crossocerus pusillus 171
Crow, Carrion 66, **80**, 81, 195

Cuckoo 62, 81
Cuckoo bumblebees 140
Cuckooflower 100
Cuculus canorus 62, 81
Culex pipiens **91**, 93
Cupressus 19
Curculio nucum 212, **213**, 215
Cyphostethus tristriatus 221, **222**, 238
Cypress 19
Cypress Pug **107**, 111, 115
Cypress, Lawson's 73, 84, 221
Cypress, Leyland 221
Cytisus scoparius 19, **19**, 24

Daddy Long-legs Spider 227, **228**, 238
Daffodil 19, 22, 24, **96**
Daisy Carpenter Bee **25**, 40, **41**, 129, **130-1**, 132-5, **132**
Daisy, Michaelmas 20, 24
Daisy, Oxeye 22, 24
Damselfly, Blue-tailed **82-3**, 88, 93
Damselfly, Common Blue 88, **90**, 93
Damselfly, Large Red 87, **89**, 93
Dance fly 186, **188**, 197
Dark Bush-cricket 219, **219**, 238
Dark-edged Bee-fly 28, **29**, 188, **188**, 197
Darter, Common 87, **87**, 93
Dasysyrphus albostriatus **181**, 196
Dasysyrphus tricinctus 181, **181**, 196
Dasysyrphus venustus 181, 196
Daucus carota 22, 24, 36, **36-7**, **136**, 148, **148**, **150**, **169**, **170**, 171, 178, **182**, 186, **193**, 194, 210, 211
Dead wood 15, 122, 123, 146, 155, **156**, **157**, 160, 167, **167**, 204, **208**, 210, 212, **213**, **214**, 235
Deer, Roe 46, **46**, 51, 54
Dendrocopos major **62**, **63**, 64, 72, 81
Dexiosoma caninum **193**, 194, 197
Didea fasciata **175**, 185, 196
Digitalis purpurea 19, **20**, **21**, 24
Dioctria baumhaueri 186, **187**, 197
Dipogon subintermedius 155, 170
Dipogon variegatus **151**, 155, 170
Dock Bug 222, **224**, 238
Dog-violet, Common 19, 24
Dolichovespula media 146, **146**, 170
Dolichovespula saxonica **146**, 170

Dolichovespula sylvestris 170
Dolycoris baccarum **216-7**, 222, 238
Dorcus parallelipipedus **206**, 209, 215
Dot (moth) 107, **108**, 115
Dove, Collared 66, 74, **77**, 81
Drinker (moth) 10
Duckweed, Common 24, 87
Dunnock **69**, 73, 74, 81
Dysdera crocata **234**, 235

Early Bumblebee **19**, 120, **139**, 140
Ectemnius cavifrons 159, 161, **163**, 171, 194
Ectemnius cephalotes 161, **164**, 171
Ectemnius continuus 159, 161, **163**, 171
Ectemnius dives 171
Ectemnius lituratus 171
Elasmucha grisea 222, 238
Elder 19, 24
Elm, English 14, 24, 98, 102
Elodea canadensis 87
Emberiza citrinella 63, 81
Emmelina monodactyla 110, **110**, 115
Empis tessellata 186, **188**, 197
Enallagma cyathigerum 88, **90**, 93
Endotricha flammealis 111, 115
Enoplognatha ovata 232, 238
Ensign fly 195, **195**, 197
Entomognathus brevis 171
Environment Agency 9
Epeolus cruciger **119**, 136, 141
Ephialtes manifestator 166, **167**, 171
Epilobium hirsutum 22, 24, 224
Epirrhoe alternata 110, **111**, 115
Epistrophe eligans **183**, 196
Epistrophe grossulariae **183**, 196
Episyrphus balteatus 30, **31**, 181, 196
Erinaceus europaeus **52**, 53, 54
Eriothrix rufomaculatus **193**, 194, 197
Eristalis arbustorum 196
Eristalis interruptus 196
Eristalis intricarius **176**, 196
Eristalis pertinax 196
Eristalis tenax **184**, 196
Erithacus rubecula **58-9**, 61, 73, **73**, 74, 81, 238
Escallonia 19, **23**, 24, **25**, 120, **135**
Euclidia glyphica 107, **111**, 115
Eupeodes corollae 181, 196

Eupeodes luniger **18,** 181, **183**, 196
Eupithecia phoeniceata **107**, 111, 115
European Ground Beetle **212**, 215
Eurrhypara hortulata 107, **112**, 115
Eurydema oleracea 238
Eurygaster testudinaria **222**, 238
Eustalomyia festiva 194,197
Eustalomyia hilaris 194, **194**, 197
Evarcha falcata **233**, 236, 238
Everlasting-pea 22, 24
Exochomus 4-pustulatus 200, **200**, 215
Eyed Hawk-moth 105, **107**, 115
Eysarcoris fabricii **222**, 238

Fairy-ring Fungus 204, **207**
Fairy-ring Longhorn 204, **207**, 215
False-acacia 14, 24, 122
Felis catus 47, 54, **54**, 61, 74
Ferdinandea cuprea 196
Field Grasshopper 219, **220**, 238
Fieldfare 80, 81
Firethorn 19, **21**, 24, 32, **32-3**, 120, 138
Fleabane, Common 22, 24, **131**, **172-3**, **193**
Flies 172-197
Flycatcher, Spotted 62, 81
Forest Bug **221**, 222, 223, 238
Forget-Me-Not 19, 24
Formica fusca 63
Forsythia 22, 24
Forsythia x intermedia 22, 24
Fourteen-spot ladybird 200, **203**, 215
Fox, Red **26**, **44-5**, 46, 48-51, **49**, **50**, 54, **55**, **56-7**, 87
Foxglove 19, **20**, **21**, 24
Fringilla coelebs 74, **75**, 76, 81
Fritillary, Dark Green 99, 114
Fritillary, Silver-washed 100, 114
Frog, Common 85, **86**, 93

Garden Bumblebee 15, **20**, 140
Garden Chafer 209, **210**, 215, **231**
Garden Slug **236**, 237-8
Garden Snail **237**, 238
Garden Spider 38, **39**, **230**, 232, 238
Garlic Mustard 100
Garrulus glandarius 61, 66, 68, 78, **78**, **79**, 81
Gasteruption assector 36, **37**, 135, 171

Gasteruption jaculator 135, **168**, 171
Gastrophysa polygoni 210, **215**, 215
Gatekeeper 100, **101**, 114
Gelis (ichneumon) 169, **169**, 171
Geranium 20, **23**, 24
German Wasp 38, **39**, 144, **146**, 170, 178, 232
Gerris lacustris 90-1, **91**, 93
Goat (moth) 178
Goldcrest **69**, 73, 81
Goldenrod 22, 24
Goldenrod, Canadian 19, 24, 40, **40-1**, **97**, 99, **110**, **119**, 132, 178, **140**, **164**, **183**
Goldfinch 63, 81
Gonepteryx rhamni 96, **96**, 114
Gonocerus acuteangulatus 220, 222, **223**, 238
Gooseberry Sawfly 171
Gorse Shieldbug **221**, 222-3, 238
Gorytes laticinctus **159**, 163, 171
Greater Bulb Fly **177**, 178, 181
Green Longhorn 115
Green Shieldbug 221, **221**, 238
Greenfinch 73, 74, **74**, 76, 81
Gull, Black-headed 81
Gull, Herring 81
Gymnomerus laevipes **155**, 170
Gymnosoma rotundatum 36, **36**, 194, 197

Habitats 12-43
Haematopota pluvialis 189, **190**, 197
Hairstreak, Brown **97**, 99, 114
Hairstreak, Purple 99, 114
Hairy Shieldbug **216-7**, 222, 238
Halictus rubicundus **122**, 141
Halictus tumulorum 141
Harlequin Ladybird 201, **204**, 215
Harmonia axyridis 201, **204**, 215
Harmonia quadripunctata 200, **202**, 215
Hawkbit, Autumn 22, 24
Hawkbit, Rough 22, 24
Hawker, Brown 88, 93
Hawker, Migrant 88, **89**, 93
Hawker, Southern 54, **88**, 87, 89, 93
Hawthorn Shieldbug **220**, 221, 238
Hawthorn, Common 19, 24, 220, 222
Hazel 212
Hazelnut Weevil 212, **213**, 215
Heather 19, 24, 38, **38-9**, 105, **111**, **113**, **119**,

120, 139, **226**, 232
Hebe 20, 24, 120, **139**, **155**
Hedera helix 24, 42, **42-3**, 98, 99, 113, **144**, **175**, 192, **195**, 232
Hedgehog **52**, 53, 54
Hedychridium roseum 36, **36**, 148, 170
Hedychrum niemelai 148, **148**, 170
Helenium hoopesii 22, 24, 132
Helianthoides scabra 22, 24, **25**, 132
Heliophanus flavipes **233**, 236, 238
Heliopsis 22, 24, **25**, 132
Helix aspera **237**, 238
Helophilus pendulus 42, **42**, 181, 196
Hepialus sylvina **109**, 115
Heracleum sphondylium 19, 24
Heriades truncorum **25**, 40, **41**, 129, **130-1**, 132-5, **132**, 141
Heron, Grey 81, 86, **92**
Heterotoma planicornis 224, **225**
Hogweed, Common 19, 24
Holly 14, 24, 98, 99
Honesty 24
Honeybee 118-20, **140**, 140
Hoplitis claviventris 141
Hoplocampa testudinea 170
Hornet 42, **43**, **144**, 145, 170, 178
Horse-chestnut 15, 24, 84, 113
Horse-chestnut Leaf Miner 113, 115
Horsefly 190, 197
House Leek 183
House Spider 227, **229**, 238
Hoverflies 174-185
Hyacinthoides x massartiana 19, 24
Hyancinthoides non-scripta 19, 24
Hydrometra stagnorum 91, **91**, 93
Hylaeus communis **119**, 129, 135, 141
Hylaeus dilatatus 141
Hylaeus hyalinatus **21**, 138, 141
Hylaeus pictipes **120**, 139, 141
Hylaeus signatus **120**, 138, 141
Hypochaeris radicata 22, 24

Iceplant 97
Ichneumon sarcitorius **166**, 168, 171
Ichneumon suspiciosus **166**, 168, 171
Ichneumon wasps 164-169
Ichneumon xanthorius 36, **37**, 168, 171

Ilex aquifolium 14, 24, 98, 99
Inachis io 96, 98, 99, **103**, 114
Iris 20, 24, 87
Ischnura elegans **82-3**, 88, 93
Ivy 24, 42, **42-3**, 98, 99, 113, **144**, **175**, 192, **195**, 232

Jackdaw **11**, 68, 70, **80**, 81, **81**, 238
Jasione montana **21**, 24
Jasmine, Winter 20, 24
Jasminum nudiflorum 24, 24
Jay 61, 66, 68, 78, **78**, **79**, 81
Juglans regia 24
Juniper 221
Juniper Shieldbug 221, **222**, 238
Jynx torquilla **62**, 63, 81

Kite, Red 61
Kite-tailed Robberfly 186, 187, 197
Knapweed, Common 22, 24
Knapweed, Greater 22, 24

Laburnum 14, 20, **20**, 24
Laburnum anagyroides 14, 20, **20**, 24
Lacewings 225
Ladybirds 200-2
Lamb's Ears 137
Larch 226
Large Rose Sawfly **169**, 171
Large Tabby 111, **112**, 115
Large Yellow Underwing **109**, 111, 115
Larus argentatus 81
Larus ridibundus 81
Lasioglossum calceatum 40, **40**,141
Lasioglossum fulvicorne 141
Lasioglossum lativentre 141
Lasioglossum minutissimum 121, 141
Lasioglossum morio **123**, 141
Lasioglossum parvulum 141
Lasioglossum punctatissimum 141
Lasioglossum smeathmanellum **15**, 121, 141
Lasioglossum villosulum 141
Lasius flavus 63
Lasius fuliginosus 63
Lasius niger 63
Lathyrus latifolius 22, 24
Lathyrus odoratus 22, 24, 212
Lavandula angustifolia 20, 24, 120, 210

Lavender, Garden 20, 24, 120, 210
Lemna minor 24, 87
Leontodon hispidus 22, 24
Leopoldius signatus 42, **43**, **191**, 192, 197
Leptophyes punctatissima **218**, 219, 238
Leptopterna ferrugata 224, **226**
Lesser Stag Beetle **206**, 209, 215
Lestiphorus bicinctus **159**, 163, 171
Leucanthemum vulgare 22, 24
Leucozona lucorum **184**, 196
Libellula depressa 88, **88**, 93
Lilac 19, 24
Lilac, Californian **20**, 22, 24, **231**, 235
Lime 107
Lime Hawk-moth 105, **107**, 115
Lindenius panzeri 171
Lissotriton vulgaris 85, **85**, 93
Damselfly, Blue-tailed **82-3**, 88, 93
Listrodromus nycthemerus **166**, 169, 171
Lotus corniculatus 24, **25**, 99, 111
Lucanus cervus 204, 206-7, **208**, 215
Lunaria annua 24
Lupin, Garden 20, 24
Lupinus polyphyllus 20, 24
Lycaena phlaeas ab. *caeruleopunctata* 99, **100**, 114

Machimus atricapillus 186, **187**, 197
Magnolia 20, 22, 24, 204
Magpie 66, 68, 70, **78**, 81, 87, 238
Mahonia aquifolium 20, 24, 30, **30-1**, **138**, **183**
Malachius bipustulatus 210, **211**, 215
Mallard 63, 81
Mallow 20, 24
Malus domestica 14, 24, **178**
Malva sylvestris 20, 24
Mammals 44-57
Maniola jurtina 100, **100**, 114
Maple, Norway 14, 24, 64, 84
Marasmius oreades 204, **207**
Marmalade Hoverfly 30, **31**, 181
Marpissa muscosa **233**, 236, 238
Marsh-marigold 20, 24, 87
May-bug 207
Mayfly 89, **91**, 93
Meconema thalassinum 219, **219**, 238
Median Wasp 146, **146**, 170

Megachile centuncularis **25**, 137, 141
Megachile ligniseca **134**, 137, 141
Megachile versicolor 137, 141
Megachile willughbiella 34, **34-5**, **135**, 137, 141
Melanchra persicariae 107, **108**, 115
Melanostoma scalare 196
Melecta albifrons **124**, 140, 141
Meles meles 46, **47**, **48**, 51-53, 54, 184
Meliscaeva auricollis 182, 196
Meliscaeva cinctella 182, **182**, 196
Melitta haemorrhoidalis 34, **35**, **125**, 141
Mellinus arvensis 161, **165**, 171, 195
Melolontha melolontha 207, **209**, 215
Merodon equestris **177**, 178, 181, 196
Mesembrina meridiana 195, **195**, 197
Micromus variegatus 225, **225**
Mignonette, Wild 22, 24, **120**
Mimas tiliae 105, **107**, 115
Mimumesa dahlbomi 160, 171
Misumena vatia **20**, **231**, 234, 238
Mole 46, 47, 48, **52**, 54
Molorchus minor 203, **205**, 215
Monosapyga clavicornis 170
Mosquito **91**, 93
Motacilla alba 80, 81
Moths 103-113
Mouse, House 46, 47, 54
Mouse, Wood 47, **53**, 54
Mus musculus 46, 47, 54
Muscicapa striata 62, 81
Myathropa florea **25**, 182, 196
Myodes glareolus 54
Myopa pellucida 190-1, **191**, 197
Myosotis 19, 24
Myrmica scabrinodis 63

Narcissus 19, 22, 24, **96**
Natrix natrix **85**, 86-7, 93
Natural England 9
Nematus ribesii 171
Netelia (ichneumon) **168**
Nettle, Stinging 18, 24, 98, 99, 102, 107
Newt, Smooth 85, **85**, 93
Noctua pronuba **109**, 111, 115
Nomada fabriciana **138**, 141
Nomada flava 141
Nomada flavoguttata 141

Nomada goodeniana 30, **30**, 141
Nomada lathburiana 141
Nomada marshamella **137**, 141
Nomada panzeri 141
Nomada ruficornis **138**, 141
Nomada signata **121**, 122, 136, 141
Nomada striata 121, **138**, 141
Noon Fly 195, **195**, 197
Notonecta glauca 90, **91**, 93
Nowickia ferox **193**, 194, 197
Nuctenea umbratica **235**, 236, 238
Nursery Web Spider 235, **236**, 238
Nuthatch **27**, **76**, 77, 81
Nysson spinosus 163, 171
Nysson trimaculatus **160**, 163, 171

Oak 10, 98, 99, 105, 158, 175, 203, 207, 211,
219, 222, 226
Oak Bush-cricket 219, **219**, 238
Oak Jewel Beetle 204, **214**, 215
Oak Roller Weevil 211, **213**, 215
Ochlodes venatus **99**, 114
Oedemera nobilis 210, **211**, 215
Oenothera 19, 24
Orange Swift **109**, 115
Orange Tip 96, **100**, 114
Oregon-grape 20, 24, 30, **30-1**, **138**, **183**
Ornithogalum umbellatum **15**, 22, 24, **121**, 138
Oryctolagus cuniculus 46, **51**, 54
Osmia bicornis **9**, 30, **31**, 124, **126-7**, 141, 151,
237
Osmia caerulescens **25**, 129, **129**, 141
Osmia leaiana **128**, 129, 141
Ourapteryx sambucaria **109**, 111, 113, 115
Owen, Dr Jennifer 10-11, 120
Owl, Tawny 47, 64, 66, 81
Oxybelus uniglumis **161**, 171

Pachygaster leachii **156**, 197
Pachytodes cerambyciformis 203, **206**, 215
Painted Lady 96, **103**, 114
Palomena prasina 221, **221**, 238
Panorpa communis 224, **225**
Panurgus calcaratus 141
Papaver 19, 24
Parakeet, Ring-necked **22**, **66**, 70-3, 81
Pararge aegeria **94-5**, 98, 114

Pardosa (spider) **235**, 237, 238
Parent Bug 222, 238
Partridge, Red-legged **64**, 81
Parus ater **71**, 74, 81
Parus caeruleus **27**, 54, **70**, **71**, 73, 74, 76, 81
Parus major 61, **72**, 73, 74, 81
Passaloecus corniger **158**, 159, 161, 171
Passaloecus gracilis 159, 171
Passaloecus singularis 171
Passer domesticus 62, **69**, 81
Passer montanus 62, 81
Passiflora incarnata 20, 24
Passion Flower 20, 24
Pea, Sweet 22, 24, 212
Peacock 96, 98, 99, **103**, 114
Pelargonium 21
Pemphredon inornata 171
Pemphredon lugubris **157**, 160-1, 166, 171
Pemphredon morio 166, 171
Pentaglottis sempervirens 22, 24
Pentatoma rufipes **221**, 222, 223, 238
Peribatodes rhomboidaria 111, **112**, 115
Perithous scurra 166, **167**, 171
Periwinkle 24
Petunia 21
Phaeostigma notata **224**, 226
Phasianus colchicus **64**, 81
Pheasant **64**, 81
Philanthus triangulum 162, **164**, 171
Phlogophora meticulosa **107**, 110, 115
Pholcus phalangioides 227, **228**, 238
Pholidoptera griseoaptera 219, **219**, 238
Phyllopertha horticola 209, **210**, 215, **231**
Phylloscopus collybita 81
Phylloscopus trochilus 62, 81
Physocephala rufipes 192, **192**, 197
Pica pica 66, 68, 70, **78**, 81, 87, 238
Picus viridis 61, 63, **64**, **65**, 70, 81
Pieris brassicae 99, 100, 114
Piezodorus lituratus **221**, 222-3, 238
Pigeon, Feral 66, 81
Pigeon, Wood 66, 73, 74, **77**, 81
Pine Ladybird 200, **200**, 215
Pinus sylvestris 185
Pipistrellus (bat) 54
Pisaura mirabilis 235, **236**, 238
Platycheirus albimanus 196

Platycheirus scutatus 196
Platypus cylindricus 204, 215
Platystomos albinus 212, **213**, 215
Plume (moth) 110, **110**, 115
Poecilobothrus nobilitatus **90**, 92, 93
Pollination 96-7,118-9
Polygonia c-album 98, 99, 102, **102**, 114
Polyommatus icarus 25, 99, 114
Pond 82-93, **84**
Pond Skater, Common 90-1, **91**, 93
Poplar, Grey 14, 24, 63
Poppy 19, 24
Populus canescens 14, 24, 63
Primrose, Evening 19, 24
Priocnemis exaltata 156, 170
Priocnemis parvula 155, 170
Priocnemis perturbator 170
Prionus coriarius 203, **205**, 215
Privet Tortrix **111**, 115
Propylea 14-punctata 200, **203**, 215
Prunella modularis **69**, 73, 74, 81
Prunus 14, 24, 28, **28-9**, **183**
Prunus laurocerasus 14, **15**, 24, 107, **178**, 202
Psenulus pallipes **158**, 161, 171
Pseudomalus auratus **147**, 150, 170
Pseudomalus violaceus 170
Pseudovadonia livida 204, **207**, 215
Psittacula krameri **22**, **66**, 70-3, 81
Psyllobora 22-punctata 200, **203**, 215
Pteridium aquilinum 24
Pulicaria dysenterica 22, 24, **131**, **172-3**, **193**
Pyracantha coccinea 19, **21**, 24, 32, **32-3**, 120, 138
Pyrausta aurata 115
Pyrausta purpuralis 107, **113**, 115
Pyrochroa coccinea 204, 215
Pyrochroa serraticornis 204, **209**, 215
Pyronia tithonus 100, **101**, 114
Pyrrhosoma nymphula 87, **89**, 93
Pyrrhula pyrrhula **8**, 61, 62, **76**, 81

Quercusia quercus 99, 114
Quince, Japanese 20, 24

Rabbit 46, **51**, 54
Ragwort, Common 19, 24, 132, **193**
Rana temporaria 85, **86**, 93

Rat, Brown 46, 47, 54
Rattus norvegicus 46, 47, 54
Red Admiral 98, **105**, 114
Red Beehive Co 123
Red Data Book 167, 175, 194, 204
Red Mason Bee **9**, 30, **31**, 124, **126-7**, 151, 237
Red-belted Clearwing 105, **106**, 115
Red-headed Cardinal Beetle 204, **209**, 215
Red-tailed Bumblebee **18**, 120, 135, **138**, 140
Redwing **68**, 80, 81
Regulus regulus **69**, 73, 81
Reseda lutea 22, 24, **120**
Rhagium bifasciatum 203, **205**, 215
Rhingia campestris 183, **185**, 196
Rhingia rostrata **172-3**, 184, **185**, 196
Rhinoceros Beetle 209, **209**, 215
Rhododendron 20, 24
Rhopalum clavipes 159, **161**, 171
Rhopalum coarctatum 159, **161**, 171
Rhyssa persuasoria 167, **167**, 171
Robin 58-9, 61, 73, **73**, 74, 81, 238
Robinia pseudoacacia 14, 24, 122
Rook 81, 195
Rosaceae 32
Rose 20, 24, 137, 220
Rosemary 211
Rosemary Beetle 210, **214**, 215
Rothamsted Research 104
Rowan 14, 24, 222
RSPB 9, 60
Rubus fruticosus 18, 24, 99
Rumex acetosa 24, 98, 99
Rutpela maculata 203, **205**, 215

Sabre Wasp 167, **167**, 171
Sage 211
Salticus scenicus **233**, 236, 238
Sambucus nigra 19, 24
Sapyga quinquepunctata **142-3**, **149**, 151, 170
Sargus bipunctatus **189**, 190, 197
Sawflies 170-1
Saxon Wasp **146**, 170
Scaeva pyrastri 175, **178**, 196
Scaeva selenitica 175, **178**, 196
Scathophaga stercoraria 194, **194**, 197

Sciurus carolinensis 46, 48, **51**, 54, 63
Scorpion Fly 224, **225**
Scorzoneroides autumnalis 22, 24
Scots Pine 185
Semaphore Fly **90**, 92, 93
Sempervivum 183
Senecio jacobaea 19, 24, 132, **193**
Sepsis (fly) 195, **195**, 197
Sericomyia silentis 42, **42**, 184, 196
Seven-spot Ladybird 28, **29**, 200, **201**, 215, **230**
Sheep's-bit **21**, 24
Shieldbugs 219-224
Short-haired Bumblebee 120
Shrew, Common 54
Sialis lutaria 91, **90**, 93
Sicus ferrugineus 34, **34**, **191**, 192, 197
Silver Y 110, **113**, 115
Sinodendron cylindricum 209, **209**, 215
Siskin **77**, 80, 81
Sitta europaea **27**, **76**, 77, 81
Sitticus pubescens **233**, 236, 238
Skimmia 20, 24
Skipper, Essex 97
Skipper, Large **99**, 114
Skipper, Small 97, 114
Sloe Bug **216-7**, 222, 238
Small Magpie (moth) 107, **112**, 115
Smerinthus ocellata 105, **107**, 115
Snail, freshwater 93, **93**
Snake, Grass **85**, 86-7, 93
Snakeflies **224**, 226
Sneezeweed 22, 24, 132
Snow 23, **26-7**
Soldier beetles **212**
Solidago canadensis 19, 24, 40, **40-1**, **97**, 99, **110**, **119**, 132, 178, **140**, **164**, **183**
Solidago virgaurea 22, 24
Sorbus aucuparia 14, 24, 222
Sorex araneus 54
Sorrel, Common 24, 98, 99
Sparrow, House 62, **69**, 81
Sparrow, Tree 62, 81
Sparrowhawk **60**, 61, **61**, 64, 81
Speckled Bush-cricket **218**, 219, 238
Speckled Longhorn 203, **206**, 215
Speckled Wood **94-5**, 98, 114

Sphaerophoria scripta 182, **182**, 196
Sphecodes ephippius **136**, 141
Sphecodes monilicornis 141
Spiders 227-237
Spilomena beata 159, **160**, 171
Spilosoma lubricipeda 104, 107, 115
Spruce Shortwing Longhorn 203, **205**, 215
Square-spot Rustic 111, **114**, 115
Squirrel, Grey 46, 48, **51**, 54, 63
St Mark's Fly 195, 197, **197**
Stachys byzantina 137
Stag Beetle 204, 206-7, **208**, 215
Starling 62, **68**, 81, **255**
Star-of-Bethlehem, Garden **15**, 22, 24, **121**, 138
Steatoda bipunctata **234**, 236, 238
Stelis breviuscula 129, **133**, 136, 141, 237
Stelis punctulatissima 136, **136**, 137, 141
Stigmus pendulus 159, **159**, 171
Stigmus solskyi 160, 171
Stiletto-fly 189, **190**, 197
Streptopelia decaocto 66, 74, **77**, 81
Stripe-legged Robberfly 186, 187, 197
Strix aluco 47, 64, 66, 81
Sturmia bella 101
Sturnus vulgaris 62, **68**, 81, **255**
Subcoccinella 24-punctata **202**, 215
Sudden Oak Death 204
Summer Chafer 207, **210**, 215
Swallow 61
Swallow-tailed Moth **109**, 111, 113, 115
Swan, Mute 61
Sweet Chestnut 105, 211
Swift 61
Swollen-thighed Beetle 210, **211**, 215
Sycamore (moth) **115**
Sylvia atricapilla 81
Sylvia borin 62, 81
Sylvia communis 81
Sylvia curruca 62, 81
Symmorphus bifasciatus **154**, 157-9, 170
Sympetrum striolatum 87, **87**, 93
Synanthedon myopaeformis 105, **106**, 115
Synanthedon vespiformis 105, **106**, 115
Syringa vulgaris 19, 24
Syritta pipiens **184**, 185, 196
Syrphus ribesii 182, 196
Syrphus vitripennis **181**, 182, 196

Tabanus bromius 197
Tachina fera **193**, 194, 197
Tachinid flies 194
Tachysphex pompiliformis 150
Talpa europaea 46, 47, 48, **52**, 54
Tanner Beetle 203, **205**, 215
Tawny Mining Bee 18, **121**, 122
Tegenaria (spider) 227, **229**, 238
Thecla betulae **97**, 99, 114
Thereva nobilitata 189, **190**, 197
Thick-headed flies 190-2
Thrush, Mistle 81
Thrush, Song 62, **67**, 73, 74, 81, 238
Thyme, Garden 22, 24, 211
Thymelicus sylvestris 97, 114
Thymus vulgaris 22, 24, 211
Tickseed 22, 24
Tiphia femorata **148**, 162, 170
Tipula paludosa 195, **196**, 197
Tit, Blue **27**, 54, **70**, **71**, 73, 74, 76, 81
Tit, Coal **71**, 74, 81
Tit, Great 61, **72**, 73, 74, 81
Tit, Long-tailed **72**, 80, 81
Toad, Common 85, **86**, 93
Tomato 232
Tortoise Bug **222**, 238
Tortoiseshell, Small 97, 98, 101, **104**, 114
Tree Bumblebee **21**, 105, 120, **138**, 140
Tree Wasp 170
Treecreeper 81
Trichrysis cyanea **148**, 150, 170
Trifolium repens 22, 24, **25**
Troglodytes troglodytes **69**, 73, 81
Troilus luridus **223**, 224, 238
Trypoxylon attenuatum 171
Trypoxylon clavicerum 156-7, **162**, 171
Trypoxylon medium 171
Turdus iliacus **68**, 80, 81
Turdus merula **27**, **67**, 73, 74, 81, 238
Turdus philomelos 62, **67**, 73, 74, 81, 238
Turdus pilaris 80, 81
Turdus viscivorus 81
Turnip Sawfly 171
Twenty-four-spot Ladybird **202**, 215
Twenty-two-spot Ladybird 200, **203**, 215
Twin-spot Centurion **189**, 190, 197
Two-banded Longhorn 203, **205**, 215

Two-spot Ladybird 200, 201, **204**, 215
Two-spot Wood-borer 204, **214**
Tyria jacobaeae 107, **108**, 115

Ulmus procera 14, 24, 98, 102
Urtica dioica 18, 24, 98, 99, 102, 107

Vanessa atalanta 98, **105**, 114
Vanessa cardui 96, **103**, 114
Varied Carpet Beetle 211, **214**, 215
Vespa crabro 42, **43**, **144**, 145, 170, 178
Vespula germanica 38, **39**, 144, **146**, 170, 178, 232
Vespula vulgaris 28, **28**, 144, **145**, 170, 178, 232
Vinca 24
Viola riviniana 19, 24
Violet Ground Beetle 209, **212**, 215
Vole, Bank 54
Volucella bombylans **176**, 178, 196
Volucella inanis 40, **41**, 178, **179**, 196
Volucella inflata 178, **179**, 196
Volucella pellucens **23**, 178, 196
Volucella zonaria 178, **179**, 196
Vulpes vulpes **26**, **44-5**, 46, 48-51, **49**, **50**, 54, **55**, **56-7**, 87

Wagtail, Pied 80, 81
Walnut 14, 24
Walnut Orb-weaver Spider **235**, 236, 238
Warbler, Garden 62, 81
Warbler, Willow 62, 81
Wasp Beetle 32, **33**, **198-9**, 215
Wasps 142-171
Water Measurer 91, **91**, 93
Waterweed, Canadian 87
White Ermine 104, 107, **108**, 115
White, Green-veined 32, **33**, **98**, 100, 114
White, Large 99, 100, 114
White, Small 100, 114
Whitebeam 222
White-tailed Bumblebee 14, 30, 38, **39**, 140
Whitethroat, Common 62, 81
Whitethroat, Lesser 62, 81
Wildlife Trusts 9
Willow 107, 122, 203
Willow Beauty 111, **112**, 115
Willowherb, Great 22, 24, 224

Wolf spider **235**, 237, 238
Woodland Trust 9
Woodlouse Spider **234**, 235
Woodpecker, Great-spotted **62**, **63**, 64, 72, 81
Woodpecker, Green 61, 63, **64**, **65**, 70, 81
Wool Carder Bee **116-7**, **136**, 137
Worcester Pearmain 14, 24
Woundwort Bug **222**, 238
Wren **69**, 73, 81
Wryneck **62**, 63, 81

Xanthogramma pedissequum 182, **183**, 196
Xestia xanthographa 111, **114**, 115
Xylota segnis 185, **186**, 196
Xylota sylvarum **186**, 196
Xysticus cristatus **231**, 238

Yarrow 22, 24, 148
Yellow Dung Fly 194, **194**, 197
Yellow Shell 107, **115**, 115
Yellowhammer 63, 81
Yellow-legged Black (soldierfly) **156**, 197
Yellow-legged Clearwing 105, **106**, 115
Yew 220

Zebra Spider **233**, 236, 238
Zicrona caerulea 223, **223**, 238
Zilla diodia **227**, 234, 238

This Starling, which appeared in March 2013, was the first seen in the garden for several years. The subtlety of the plumage stands out

Nature is better at recycling than humans will ever be and ants are among the best in the business. Here a worker shows phenomenal strength heading for the nest with a paralysed spider mislaid by a spider-hunting wasp